RASA SINGAPURA
TASTE OF SINGAPORE
With Vegetarian Conversion

Singapore has been [...] t. Food centres, with hu[...]g from satay to bacon-a[...] or in the basements of shopping cen[...]es. Together with the 24-hour coffee houses and restaurants, they provide a quality and variety of food that is staggering; Asian cuisine exists in abundance alongside its Western counterpart. Nowhere in the world is there such diversity with such low prices.

Eating in Singapore is so much a way of life that the informal greeting, in any of the four official languages (i.e, English, Malay, Chinese and Tamil) is, "Have you eaten?"

Visitors to this tiny island-nation often remark on first, its pristine cleanliness, and second on the sense of smell: the aroma of freshly prepared food rising to mingle with the scent of frangipanis, roses and jasmine.

Rasa Singapura/Taste of Singapore

Rasa is the Malay word for 'to taste' or 'to feel'. Therefore this book attempts to paint a gastronomic picture of this tropical isle so that you may taste the foods which are a result of the harmonious mingling of the cosmopolitan races that make up the Singaporeans. Through snippets of information about this country which was once part of the British Empire, it is also hoped that you will feel its unique atmosphere and imbibe its spirit.

Humble Beginnings

Sir Stamford Raffles put Singapore on the world map when he bought Singapore from the Temmengong of Johore in 1819 as a trading post for the East India Company. At that time, the island was called Singapura, a sanskrit word that meant Lion City (Singa=Lion, Pura=City). In acquiring this swampy, fishing village and recognising the island's strategic position as a port of call between the West and the East, the far-sighted English clerk inadvertently became the catalyst in fulfilling the prophesy made by a legendary prince of Indonesia.

Apparently, the prince who was called Sang Nila Utama had seen the sandy, golden beach that fringed the island of Temasek from his hill-top palace. Its gleaming beauty and swaying palm trees seemed to beckon him and so he set across the waters with his courtiers. They discovered only a handful of indigenous Malays living there.

When the royal party swathed through the thick undergrowth, they came across an animal as regal as the prince. Startled by their presence, the animal bounded off with immeasurable grace. Having not seen such a creature before, with its proud carriage and mane of reddish hair, the prince enquired after its name.

"It's a *singa*/lion, my lord," he was told.

Overwhelmed by the majesty of the animal, the prince then pronounced, "I shall call this island, Singa-Pura." Nobody of course liked to remind the prince that the island already had a name.

"It will be a great city someday!" Sang Nila Utama enthused.

Today modern Singapore is indeed a great metropolis. But not one filled merely with concrete blocks. Flowering shrubs, trees and parks vie with sky-scrapers for supremacy in what came to be called a garden-city.

Is There Such A Thing As Singaporean Cuisine?

Because of its youth, the nation of Singapore is still struggling to produce a National Persona from its multi-racial community. Ethnic groups, being encouraged to pursue their own languages and culture also breed a kind of separateness although they will swear that they are Singaporeans first and being Chinese, Malay, Indian or Eurasian, second.

In the same way, no one cuisine can be classed as the Singaporean cuisine although there is an emergence of a particular style of preparation of the foods it shares with its neighbouring nations of Malaysia and Indonesia; for example: satay, nasi-goreng, rendang, curries etc., which would be recognisable as Singaporean.

Peranakan/Nonya Cuisine (Straits Chinese Cuisine)

This requires a special mention because the Straits Chinese (or Peranakans, as we call ourselves) have a unique cuisine

born out of the exotic marriage between the Malay and the Chinese. Our cuisine, like our culture, is an integration of the cuisine and culture of the two different races. The females of our race are called nonyas, hence our cuisine tends to be commonly known as Nonya Cuisine and is often spoken of in exalted terms as the cordon bleu of Asian cuisine.

(Legend has it that Peranakans were born from the marriage between the Chinese Princess, Hang Li Po and the Malay Sultan Mansur Shah. He was then the ruler of the principality of Malacca and she was the daughter of the Emperor of Ancient Cathay. The marriage was a purely political move by the Emperor to secure the control of the Straits of Malacca since Malacca was an important port of call between the East and West, long before Singapore replaced it. The princess also took to Malacca her retinue of handmaidens and courtiers and they too intermarried with the indigenous Malays as did the merchants who traded there. Eventually some of these people migrated to Singapore and Penang. These three places were named the Straits Settlements by the British and that was how the words 'Straits Chinese' came about. This term differentiates us from the Overseas Chinese who remain Chinese in thought and culture although they are away from their motherland.)

Due to the culinary marriage of the Malay and Chinese cuisine, Nonya Cuisine can be described as Chinese cuisine that has been malayanised. Ingredients such as *serai*/lemon grass, *lengkuas*/galangal, unused in Chinese cuisine, are the most identifiable ingredients of Nonya food. They are aromatic and give a unique flavour to the dishes.

My mother gave me these recipes when I was knee high, as her mother had done before her. As eldest daughter, I was expected to know how to cook and sew.

Extinction Of A Race

Sadly, my generation would probably be the last of the real Peranakans. These days, Singaporeans with Chinese extraction are deemed Chinese and must take Chinese as their second language in school – the Peranakan creole and customs will soon be lost. Nearly all Peranakans have married non-Peranakan partners, so after the death of this generation of Peranakans, there'll be no one left to testify to our existence. There have been attempts to write about us and even a museum was set up in our honour but it is apparent that we are being assimilated into the larger group of Chinese.

Why A Cook-Book For The West?

Problems arise when one picks up a cook-book, say of Singaporean Cooking from Singapore. When the book is written for its own country, it utilises all the available ingredients of that country.

This book tries to create as authentic a Singaporean cuisine as possible using the spices and ingredients that are easily available in the west. For example, fresh coconut is not so easily available. And even if it is, the coconut tends to be much older than the type that would be used in Asia and therefore the quantity and quality of its milk is affected.

Thus, there must be adjustments in the recipes that cater for these differences to make cooking a foreign food an enjoyable task.

Vegetarian Conversion

So many people turn to vegetarianism for all sorts of reasons. Non-vegetarians seem to think that vegetarians have boring meals. This is not at all necessary. With a bit of imagination, any dish can be created to make it into a vegetarian one. At the end of each recipe, I have shown how each dish can be converted to suit the vegetarian. Therefore this book is suitable for both the vegetarian and non-vegetarian and particularly useful for the carnivore who has a vegetarian for a partner or vice-versa (see Item 11 of Tips And Information).

So, Rasa Singapura!
Have a Feel And Taste Of Singapore
right in your own kitchen. Selamat Makan!
Safe (Happy) Eating!

I. Tips And Information

A good combination in a Singaporean meal consists of both spicy and non-spicy dishes so that the palate is not deluged with spices. The base of most of the 'sauces', to use a European-type term, is made up of onions and garlic, sometimes with ginger. In Asia, it is believed that onions help to dispel excess 'wind' in the abdominal tract so that one is free from indigestional problems. Garlic, on the other hand is reputed to be an aphrodisiac. Today, western doctors have also attributed it to be a great factor in dissolving cholesterol, especially around the heart.

By cooking both onions and garlic in the method described in this book, their aftertaste will not be felt or smelled.

1 Rice

Rice is the best accompaniment to most of the recipes in this book. However, curries or anything with sauces can also be eaten with crusty bread, like a french loaf or rolls. This will be stipulated in each recipe.

In its natural state, rice is grown in sheafs, like wheat. It requires a great deal of water to grow in, therefore they grow in padi-fields, flooded with water. In English, the same word applies whether the rice is cooked or uncooked but in Malay, uncooked rice is called *padi*.

A grain of rice is enclosed in a husk so white rice has been de-husked and polished. The grade of brown rice therefore depends on how much sifting and polishing the rice has gone through. Brown rice is of course more nutritious and is good for roughage. Although brown rice has more flavour, it is debatable whether it is more palatable, especially to Asians. Very few Asians would eat brown rice regularly, except for the health-conscious because for generations, brown rice was eaten by the poor since they could not afford the process of having their rice polished. (What sins we commit in the name of civilisation!) Another reason was that brown rice was also used as a major animal-feed.

2 Coconut Rice/Nasi Lemak

Instead of cooking rice with water, you can use coconut milk. The measurement of coconut milk/cream is the same as that of water. However, you need to add a little salt as well. The fragrance of rice cooked in this way is mouth-watering! In the East this is often eaten as a breakfast with fresh fried fish, sambal/chilli, a piece of omelette and cucumber.

3 Rice Porridge/Moey

When you put in too much water and the rice turns soggy, don't despair, it has become what we call, rice porridge! Unlike the English rice pudding, this is cooked in water till it becomes a watery gruel and is eaten with savoury dishes like any of the dishes in this book. In Teochew, one of the dialects of Chinese, it is called Moey. It is very convenient for babies and old people who have problems with their teeth, or patients who are convalescing as it is more easily digestible. Moey is one of the 'cooling' type of dish and so is excellent when you're feeling too hot and bothered or when you have a sore throat, fever etc. It could also be cooked with bits of fish, meat or vegetables with a raw egg thrown in it so that it becomes a one-dish meal where all the nutrients are in the same dish.

4 Curry Powder And Spices

There seems to be a misconception that curry powder is some kind of mystical concoction. It is really only a mixture of specific spices made into a sauce. When the proportion of these spices vary, you end up with different types of curries for example, madras, vindaloo, meat/fish curry etc.

The spices are taken whole, then ground resulting in 'powder' which is easier to keep. In wet-markets (as opposed to supermarkets) in Asia, you still find Curry-Powder Sellers who would grind the spices fresh each day on a Batu Giling, an equipment like a rolling pin and a slab, except that they are made of granite. A little water is added to the dry spices and the grinding turns them into a kind of paste. The flavour of the curry when cooked with such a paste makes your mouth water so much, it is unbelievable!

Another way of increasing the flavour of your curry is to dry-fry the coriander and cummin seeds without oil, before grinding them. I still try to do this although as far as the Batu Giling is concerned, I've given it up for the less arduous, blender.

So, you can create your own curry powder by combining the different spices. Here is one example so that you can make up your own in due course by decreasing or increasing the amount of chilli and pepper. The advantage of having the desired combination made-up and stored is that you can simply spoon out a couple of tablespoonfuls when you need it instead of trying to mix the spices each time you want to do a curry.

For approximately 500gm of curry powder:

200gm ground coriander	75gm ground aniseed
50gm ground cummin	50gm ground black or
75gm ground chilli powder	white pepper
1 tsp ground cinnamon	2 tsp ground turmeric
1 tsp ground cloves	1 tsp ground cardamon

Keep your curry powder in a air-tight jar. You need approximately 2 tablespoonful of curry powder to be mixed into a paste (See II, *Item 4*) for 4 persons. If you love your own concoction, you can use this instead of the proportions suggested in the recipes in this book.

5 Chillis

Don't be deceived by its colour! There are red, yellow and green chillis. In Singapore, the milder ones tend to be green but I have discovered that this is not always true in the west. As a rule of thumb, the smaller and slimmer the chillis are, the hotter they are. There is a small one-inch sized chilli in the East (which tends to be green) but it is so hot that it can make you smoke! It is called a chilli-padi (because it is small like a grain of rice). Hence its name is also given to someone who is small in stature but dynamic.

A main criticism hurled at the usage of chillis is that it blunts the taste-buds. Any lover of chillis will tell you that this is totally untrue. To the uninitiated, it may seem like it fires up the palate but what it does is to open up the 'pores' of the taste-buds, making you salivate more. We call this a cleansing of the palate after which one can appreciate the subtler taste of food.

Most of the recipes in this book call for the use of dried or chilli-powder. There are two reasons for this: (i) Fresh chilli seem to be more difficult to get than its dried variety (But if you can get them, fine, just use them in place of the dried); (ii) There seems to be such an inconsistent strength of the various types of chillis in the west that it would be hard to say 'use 2 chillis' when 2 chillis could blow one's mind one day and be too mild another. So I have left the adventure of discovery to yourself.

How To Use Chillis
If using fresh chillis to make into a sauce, you need to slice them first before putting into the blender. As for dried chillies, you need to soak them in boiling water for 2-3 minutes, take them out of the water and blend.

If using chilli powder, always add a few drops of water to make it into a paste and then fry so that there is no powdery taste.

Whether using fresh or dried chillis, removing their seeds will automatically reduce its 'tang'.

6 Coconut Cream And Substitutes
Fresh coconuts are so easily available in Singapore. Not only that, they are also sold freshly grated. That is why so many dishes are prepared with this wonderfully fragrant commodity.

Contrary to some erroneous beliefs, coconut milk is not contained in the space inside the kernel. Inside this space is coconut-water. In very young, green coconuts, this water makes a very refreshing drink but it is discarded in older coconuts. To get coconut milk, the kernel has to be scraped off its shell and then grated. A little water is added to the grated coconut and then squeezed to let the milk out. Unfortunately, no coconut cream, powder or milk that are in cans can even come near to the delicious taste of fresh coconut milk.

Another undeserving label the coconut has received is that it is high in cholesterol. It is true that a coconut contains a certain amount of fat but it is only natural, vegetable oil. (Dried coconut kernels are called copras. When pressed, these copras release coconut oil.)

Fresh kernel is delicious and can be eaten on its own. It is often grated and made into Nonya Cakes. (Actually puddings would be a more appropriate term than cake.)

Using Fresh Coconut Milk
When squeezing the milk from a fresh coconut, one normally separates the milk into two lots: the first lot being called *pati-santan* or coconut cream and the second, *santan* or just coconut milk. (The Malay word for coconut is *kelapa*.) This is because the cream contains a lot more fat and therefore is put into the sauce last. When you boil coconut milk over heat, the fat will break out from the coconut, too much of this will spoil the sauce. That is why, the heat is usually turned down once the coconut milk is added. Having said this, substitutes like coconut cream block, powder etc does not produce such a great effect. Single creams are often quite good as substitutes in recipes that require coconut milk.

7 Desserts
There are no recipes for desserts in this book.

One main reason is that Singaporean desserts depend quite heavily on the flavour of fresh coconut and I have discovered that in this instance, single cream is not a good substitute. Another thing is that the so-called desserts or sweets of Singapore tend to be heavy and stodgy using lots of glutinous or pudding rice. Therefore they are highly unsuitable as 'afters'. Besides, Asians do not have desserts in the same way as Westerners. Usually the meal is finished with a 'mouth-cleanser' with fresh fruits like papaya, pineapples or oranges.

Therefore 'sweets' are eaten as snacks. The average Singaporean eats three main meals a day. Most people would include another, a light supper. However, in between meals, they would eat these Nonya Cakes or 'sweets' or curry-puffs (like small pasties) with their afternoon coffee or tea.

8 Aromatic Roots: Lemon Grass And Galangal
Of the two, lemon grass or serai has the more distinct flavour and taste although both complement each other. Galangal is sometimes called Blue Ginger. The former is more easily available here than the latter.

To use the lemon grass, cut off the grass and greenish part of the stalk, use only the whitish root. This root can be merely bruised and dropped into the sauce or more often, sliced and then blended with the onions and garlic to make up the sauce. *Lengkuas*/Galangal is also used in this way except that the skin should be first taken off.

9 Type Of Oil Used
Of course you can use any type of fat you prefer in cooking but in Asian cooking, usually corn, vegetable, soya or peanut oil is used. We tend to keep to the polyunsaturates or unsaturates which are healthier for you anyway. Sesame oil is sometimes recommended for specific dishes because of its fragrance.

10 Cuts Of Meat
No specific cut of meat is mentioned in the recipes although for quick-cooking the leaner meats are advisable. In curries and sauces that take longer to

cook, you can have a choice of cuts though you must remember that if you need to simmer a long time, do not add the coconut cream till last.

11 Vegetarian Conversion

Each recipe ends with a vegetarian conversion. In the standard recipe *V indicates that a vegetarian conversion is available. The amount of the substitute ingredient is given as if the vegetarian dish is catered to the same number of persons as indicated in the standard menu. This is done to facilitate explanation.

However, you can divide one standard recipe for both a vegetarian as well as a non-vegetarian. For example, if you wish to do Minced Beef With Peas *(Mb1)* which is for 4 persons and you have one vegetarian guest, you need not do a separate dish. Instead of the full portion of 250 gm minced quorn, use 75 gm or as per your discretion. Work the recipe as per normal but before you put in the beef, take out a portion of the sauteed spices and onion/garlic mix to put into a separate saucepan. Then just allocate a third portion of the remaining ingredients to the vegetarian dish and finish off as you would the standard recipe. This saves a lot of bother and makes the meal interesting for the vegetarian.

The substitutes for meats used in this cook-book are:

a) **Quorn.** It is a myco-protein food made from a tiny plant. Does not contain any cholesterol and is full of dietary fibre. Comes in bite pieces. It has no flavour on its own and takes it from sauces.

b) **Tofu,** of Chinese origin. It is made from soya beans and made into a cake. Usually, there are three consistencies, normal tofu, firm, extra firm. Silken tofu is much more delicate than the firm beancurd type, hence is harder to handle. Tofu can be used as it is or sauteed first to give it a layer of skin. If you like, marinate with 1 tsp of turmeric powder and 1 tsp of chilli powder before sauteeing. This gives it extra flavour.

c) **Tempeh,** of South East Asian origin. It is made from whole soya beans, fermented like cheese and compressed into a cake. It has a nutty, crunchy taste. It is very crumbly and therefore when rubbing spices into it, care has to be taken.

d) **Soya Mince/Soya Burger Mix/Soya Sausage Mix**
Where soya mince is required, any of the above will be appropriate. (Note that the recipe will say burger/sausage mix as it is obvious that it will be soya as it comes under the vegetarian conversion). Do remember to hydrate the soya and then work from recipe as if it was fresh mince. Some soya mince are not flavoured nor seasoned while others are; so do work wisely and reduce salt and seasoning or increase them as the case may be. (To cheat, I use ready-made soya or tofu burgers.)

e) **Quail Eggs** – because they are small, they can be easily coated with any sauce. Most of the time, they should be hard-boiled and then shelled before using in recipe. For vegans, stick to any of the three mentioned above.

12 Soup

A soup is not served as a separate course as in Western meals. Traditionally, it is served as part of the combination of a whole meal, particularly when all the other dishes in the combination lack sauce. Therefore an Asian soup is always thin. Basically it is used to 'wet' the rice. In less formal occasions, the soup is contained in a large soup tureen placed in the middle of the dining table and everyone dips their spoon in this for their share. In more formal occasions, side bowls are given to individual diners.

II. Terms Used in The Book

To avoid ambiguity, I am just clarifying some of the terms used in the book:

1 Heat

As the cooking tends to be quick, heat is usually turned up high from the beginning. However, you will be asked to turn down the heat when necessary.

2 Blend

You will come across this term very often. Usually onions and garlic are blended together. The idea is to get a fine, mushy mix so that the sauce is smooth. To get a mixture which is a good base for a smooth sauce, add a little water. But this must be allowed to dry up in the pan/wok before adding any oil. (In the recipe, therefore, it will ask you to 'allow excess liquid to dry up'.) Naturally, before onions, ginger, chillies etc can be blended, they need to be sliced first to give the blades lesser work.

It is important to saute this mixture well to eradicate the aftertaste of onion and garlic. Saute till the mixture turns slightly brownish is a good guide as to the length of time you need to saute it.

3 Pound

This is done with a mortar-and-pestle. This is suggested when the quantity of the ingredient is too small to warrant the use of a blender e.g a clove of garlic.

In recipes that require peanuts to be used, blending might do too fine a job so pounding would be better as it leaves the nut crunchy without becoming too pasty.

4 Make Into A Paste

You are normally asked to do this with the various ground spices in the recipe. This is another very common term used in the book.

Very simply, take a small dish or bowl and put in all the various spices stipulated, add a few drops of water and stir with a spoon to get a ball of paste. If you have not got enough water, the spices will not come together in a lump; if you have too much, it will get too watery.

If you do not add water to the spices before you fry them, you will burn them easily. Another important reason is that unfried spice-powder will taste floury and leave an after-taste in your mouth.

5 Fry Till Fragrant
If you do not fry the spice-paste till fragrant, you will still end up with that floury feeling. When there is sufficient oil in the wok/pan, you can fry the paste without it sticking, the paste will brown slightly and a wonderful aroma will arise.

6 'Simmer Gently Until Oil Has Separated From Cream'
With either coconut or fresh cream, the fat content will be released when the sauce is heated. If the heat is too high, this occurs too quickly and spoils the sauce. Hence, you are always asked to turn down the heat as soon as you have added the cream.

Separation takes place when little blobs of oil appear in the sauce and the sauce will thicken. This means that the spices/chillies and cream have reached its optimum stage of mingling.

7 'Remove From Oil' And 'Remove Entirely'
This may seem like a redundant instruction but I am aware that some people may not have seen how the finished dish should look like and therefore cannot tell if the oil forms part of the sauce or otherwise. So as a precaution, the recipe will state, 'Remove Entirely' when the oil that the chicken was done in forms part of the sauce; or 'Remove From Oil' when the chicken should be dished out without the oil.

8 Marshalling Area
This is the area which is within reach from where you would be standing once you have started cooking. Prepare all the required ingredients, including measuring out everything that is needed and put them in small dishes or dinner-size plates and 'marshall' them in this area so that you have everything at hand.

9 Coconut Cream
In this book, the measure is for coconut cream powder. This is because this is more easily available and easy to use. If you are familiar with the cream block type, do carry on with it but be careful not to pour boiling water to dissolve it otherwise the oil will separate from it too soon.
I personally prefer canned coconut milk or powder to the block.

To use the cream powder, measure the amount as stated then pour warm water over it to make into liquid. Use from liquid state. If cream powder is of poorer, less creamy quality, add one tbsp single cream to enhance taste.

10 Stock
Whenever possible, make use of freshly made vegetable or meat stock. However, in this book, stock cubes or dried veg stock are recommended to make it easier. By all means use your homemade stock for better flavour.

11 Preparation/Cooking Time
This presumes that you have everything ready in your marshalling area before you begin cooking. Of course timing is based on my personal experience. This hopes to serve as a guide not a race.

III. Serving A Singaporean Meal

1 Serving The Meal
In general, the only thing that is on the dinner plate itself would be the rice. All other dishes are placed on the table, each with a serving spoon so that your guest can help himself to the food. Your guest is thus free to choose what he wishes to taste or eat.

Note: The rice is not placed in the middle of the dinner plate, it should be placed on the lower half of the plate nearest the diner. Whatever you take from the dishes on the table are then arranged in a semi-circle on the top half of the plate, they are not put directly on the rice. This gives you the facility of checking out the taste of each dish without mixing up the flavours. And the polite way is to mix only small portions of the rice each time.

No Division Of Starters And Main Course
Only during a banquet are dishes served in courses. Otherwise, in a Singaporean meal, there is no division between starter and main courses. Restaurants in the West have of course adopted the western style of eating but in Singapore, soups are served at the same time as main courses. Sometimes little bowls are set beside your dinner plate with its own spoon for your soup. But during family dinners, there is only a huge bowl of soup in the middle of the table from which everyone dips their spoon.

2 Eating With Fingers
Us traditional Straits Chinese, Malays and Indians use our fingers to eat rice at home (and in some restaurants which supply banana leaves instead of plates) but would use fork and spoons when eating out.

It is considered not only an art to eat properly with fingers, it is a also a very sensual experience. People who eat regularly with fingers find such great pleasure in the taste of the food that they will swear that the use of forks and spoons or any other instrument detracts from the sensuality of eating! (They argue that the sense of touch heightens the eating experience in the same way as in love-making; surely the touch of a warm hand is much more pleasurable than a gloved one?)

Traditionally, we use our right hands for eating and left ones for ablutions. It is quite obvious that hands must be washed clean and for efficacy, fingernails are better kept short. Finger bowls are often provided at tables and a squeeze of lime added to the water. Except for some types of Indians who enjoy rolling their rice into a ball in the palms of their hands, most of us do not get our palms soiled. In fact, we really only use our fingertips but up to the second joints is permissible.

The secret of the technique is to keep the four fingers as close to one another as possible so that they do not become splayed and thus spilling the food. Mix the curry

or sauce into the rice with the fingers. Bend your fingers to create a kind-of-scoop, raise them to your lips. As you open your mouth, gently push the food into your mouth with your thumb. (Your fingers must remain together so that the fingers are not pointing upwards as this is considered unmannered.)

IV. Singaporean Eating Habits And Health

Eating is the past-time of Singapore. It is extremely rare to come across a Singaporean on a diet. In general, people eat three main meals and a fourth, lighter meal for supper. Out of the four meals, perhaps one or two meals would be cooked at home. Hawker or food centres supply all the other meals.

Food/Hawker Centres

They were called hawker centres because itinerant hawkers used to push their carts to an open ground or car-park to ply their trade in unison. The most famous one was at The Carpark on Orchard Road which has long gone, replaced by high-rise buildings. These days, there are no itinerant hawkers and stall holders ply their trade outdoors or in the basement level of offices and shopping centres. They comprise of some twenty to fifty stalls selling a variety of foods from noodles, to rice to steaks. Meals are ordered at individual stalls and are served at numbered tables where you pay for your food. There are no tips involved and food is cheap and cooked fresh! Well known tourist hawker centres include the ones at Newton Circus and Satay Club which are both outdoors. Those along the East Coast serve wonderful fresh-caught seafood. If you get an opportunity to visit Singapore, ask Singaporeans for local food/hawker centres where prices are not too high.
(Or write/fax/e-mail me for suggestions.)

Cooling And Heaty Foods

The Yin-And-Yang principle exists in every aspect of Chinese life in Singapore. It takes different forms in the other ethnic philosophy but the same principle is present.

This principle of balance and harmony is also taken into foods. Therefore foods are classed 'heaty' or 'cooling' in the way that they will affect the body. For example fried foods are considered heaty while fruits and vegetables are considered cooling. Excess of heaty foods give rise to ailments like sore-throats and fevers, while excess of cooling foods result in colds, low resistance etc.

Exercise

Singaporeans are fortunate in that the equatorial climate encourages out-door living. With the resulting affluence, people can afford to engage in all sorts of sports like sailing, water-skiing, wind-surfing etc. people can swim, play tennis and squash till late into the evenings.

Traditional Eastern exercises are different from the western because they tend to be holistic in nature, catering not only to the physical body but to the mental and emotional health of the individuals as well. Such systems include Tai Chi, Yoga, Kung Fu etc whose main objective is the regulation of the 'life force' or energy that comes from within. When this life force is depleted, dis-ease i.e. disease results.

Yoga regulates the lifeforce or energy that comes from within.

If you are an early riser in Singapore, you can see groups of people practising Tai Chi Chuan outdoors, in parks, on badminton courts etc. Their movements are slow and languid, one flowing into the other as they try to get in touch with nature and themselves. It is indeed a lovely sight.

RASA SINGAPURA

TASTE OF SINGAPORE

With Vegetarian Conversion

MINCED BEEF WITH PEAS
KEEMA *(Ref: Mb 1)*

Spiced minced beef cooked in its own juice with tomato and peas
Preparation Time: 10 mins. Cooking Time: 20 mins
(4 persons)

INGREDIENTS
500 gm minced beef *V
200 gm peas
3 medium size onions
2 level tbsp gr. coriander
1 level tbsp gr. cummin
1 1/2 level dsp hot chilli powder
1 level tsp gr. black pepper
a pinch of gr. cardamon
a pinch of gr. cinnamon

} *Add a few drops of water to make into a thick paste.*

2 tomatoes
4 tbsp coconut cream
1 beef stock cube *V
1 level dsp cornflour
3 tbsp veg. oil
150 ml. water
salt to taste

MAIN UTENSILS
Blender, pan or
wok with lid

METHOD
Slice onions. Halve, then quarter tomatoes. Put on plate. Prepare spice paste as above. In a cup, put in cornflour and add water to make thin paste. Measure out all other ingredients into individual, small dishes and take everything to marshalling area.

Pour oil into pan/wok over heat. When oil is heated, put in onions and saute till soft and slightly brown. Immediately add spice paste and stir till fragrant. Add minced beef. Stir continuously till mince has absorbed spices. Then add water and stock-cube and salt. Cover for 1/2 minute.

Uncover. Put in tomato pieces, peas, cornflour paste and coconut cream. Turn heat to low. When gravy is thick, spice mixture will cling to mince, then it's ready. Remove entirely from wok. Serve hot with Roti Jala Cs 2, crusty bread or rice.

Traditionally this dish is eaten with fingers. Break off crepe or bread and scoop up mince. Also good as a filler for jacket potatoes.

> ### VEGETARIAN CONVERSION
> **V, use 250 gm of minced Quorn.*
> *Substitute *V, vegetable stock in place of meat stock.*

SLIVERS OF BEEF
IN DRY CURRY PASTE
RENDANG *(Ref: Mb 2)*

Most popular of Singaporean food – the flavour of beef captured in aromatic spices with a blend of coconut
Preparation Time: 20 mins. Cooking Time: 20 mins
(4 persons)

INGREDIENTS
500 gm lean meat *V
1 medium size onion
3 cloves garlic
2 cm length blue/ ordinary ginger
1 lemon grass

} *Put in blender and add a little water to get a smooth mixture = Mix 'A'*

1 level tbsp hot chilli powder
2 level tbsp gr. coriander
1 level tbsp gr. cummin
1/2 level tsp gr. cinnamon
1/4 level tsp gr. cloves
1/2 level tsp gr. nutmeg
1/2 level tsp gr. turmeric

} *Add a few drops of water to make into a thick paste, = Mix 'B'*

2 level tbsp freshly grated or dessicated coconut
4 tbsp coconut cream
1 sprig of fresh coriander leaves
1 tsp honey or sugar
150 ml water
4 tbsp veg oil
salt to taste

MAIN UTENSILS
Blender, pan or wok with lid

METHOD
Clean beef and slice into thin but wide slivers, (Approx 1/2x8cm) Set aside on plate. Prepare Mix 'A' and 'B' in separate bowls. Put grated/dessicated coconut and coriander leaves into blender to get Mix 'C'. Measure out all other ingredients and take to marshalling area.

Put pan/wok over heat without any oil. Put in Mix 'A' and stir to get rid of excess liquid. Then add in oil and saute till slightly brown. Add Mix'B' and fry till fragrant. Add meat and salt, stir well to coat meat with spices before adding water. Pour in water and cover for 2 mins.

Uncover. Stir well. Add honey/sugar, coconut cream and Mix 'C'. Turn heat to medium. Continue stirring. Sauce should thicken and cling to meat. When oil has broken away from cream, remove entirely. Serve hot with boiled rice, Roti Jala or bread.

> ### VEGETARIAN CONVERSION
> **V, use 250 gm Quorn, slice each cube of Quorn thinly to allow for greater absorption. Add veg.stock to improve taste.*

BEEF RISSOLES IN SOYA SAUCE
TIMPRA LEMBU *(Ref: Mb 3)*

Rissoles of beef gently simmered in lemon juice and soya sauce
Preparation Time: Sauce is prepared when rissoles are being grilled. Cooking Time: 20 mins
(2 persons)

INGREDIENTS

Rissoles:
200 gm minced beef *V
1 egg yolk, size A1
1 level tsp gr. black pepper
1 level dsp beef seasoning *V
1 level dsp cornflour
salt to taste
oil for greasing tray

Sauce:
1 onion, medium size
2 cloves garlic
2 fresh chillies or 1/2 red pepper
(to provide colour without the tang)
2 tbsp rich soya sauce
1 dsp fresh lemon juice
1 level dsp cornflour
1/2 tsp gr. black pepper
1 tsp honey
250 ml water
1 tbsp sesame oil

MAIN UTENSILS
Baking tray, grill, pan/wok

METHOD

Put all ingredients for rissoles in a bowl. Mix thoroughly. Scoop out one dessertspoonful and form into rissoles. Makes 10. Grease a baking tray and put under grill at maximum heat. Approx. 7 mins on first side, turn over, 3 mins on the next.

While the rissoles are under the grill, prepare for the sauce. Slice onions and chillies/red pepper. Crush garlic. Put cornflour into a cup to make a watery paste. Measure out all other ingredients and take to marshalling area.

Heat oil in pan/wok over maximum heat. When oil is fragrant, saute garlic. Quickly add sliced onions and chillies. Saute till limp. Pour in water, soya sauce, lemon juice, pepper and honey. When sauce boils, put in cooked rissoles and cornflour paste. Allow sauce to thicken and remove entirely from pan/wok. Serve hot with boiled rice or rice porridge.

> *VEGETARIAN CONVERSION*
> **V,100 gm of soya mince/Veg.Sausage/Burger Mix. Hydrate.*
> *If already seasoned, do not season again.*
> *Grill 5 mins on first side.*

ROLLED MINCED BEEF
KOFTA *(Ref: Mb 4)*

Marinated minced beef, deftly rolled and grilled to perfection
Preparation Time: 20 mins. Cooking Time: 10 mins
(4 persons)

INGREDIENTS

500 gm minced beef *V
2 onions, medium size
3 egg yolks, size A1
1 level dsp hot chilli powder
1 level dsp gr. coriander
1 level dsp gr. cummin
1/4 level tsp gr. turmeric
1/2 level tsp gr. black pepper
1 level dsp cornflour
1 level dsp chopped fresh coriander leaves
salt to taste
oil for greasing tray

MAIN UTENSILS
Skewer or chopstick, baking tray, grill

METHOD

Chop onions till fine. (Use blender if you like but do not make them mushy so that crunchiness is maintained.) Put mince in a bowl and add chopped onions and all the other ingredients. Mix thoroughly. Consistency should be stiff.(If required, add more cornflour)

Use a skewer or chopstick to roll mince. (The thicker the stem of the skewer/chopstick, the larger the hollow will be. But if hollow is too big, it will collapse). Wash hands well. Take a dessertspoonful of mince mixture in your right hand, flatten, then wrap around skewer/chopstick. Spread mince over 10 cm length. Ease kofta out. Makes 20. Grill for 7 mins on first side and 3 mins on the next.

Serve as a snack on its own with salad. If serving with rice, it would be a good idea to complement it with a dish that has a sauce.

> *VEGETARIAN CONVERSION*
> **V, use 250 gm. soya mince or Veg. Sausage Mix.(Sausage Mix is more suitable than Burger Mix here because it clings better.) Hydrate.*
> *Require more cornflour to make the mince hold together. It is not as easy to roll soya mince or Veg. Sausage Mix. Keep consistency firm.*
> *Don't worry too much about achieving hollow in Veg. kofta.*

CORNED BEEF HASH
A LA SINGAPORE
(Ref: *Mb 5*)

A handy recipe to have when you run out of fresh meat
Preparation Time: 3 mins. Cooking Time: 18 mins
(2 persons)

INGREDIENTS

200 gm corned beef (either loose or canned) *V
1 onion, medium
2 fresh chillies (Or 1/2 red pepper to get
colour without the tang)
1 tsp gr. black pepper
2 tbsp veg oil

MAIN UTENSIL
pan or wok

> ### CAUTION!
> NOT GLUTEN-FREE

METHOD

Slice onions and chillies (or pepper). Put corned beef in a bowl and rake well with fork. Heat oil in pan/wok over heat. Saute onions and chillies till soft. Add corned beef and fry well, taking care to break up lumps. Add gr. black pepper. When the corned beef turned slightly crispy, remove from oil.

Serve hot in a sandwich or with boiled rice or rice porridge.

> *VEGETARIAN CONVERSION*
> *There is no vegetarian substitute for corned beef as the flavour is nor imitable. *V, use 100 gm of soya mince, Veg.Sausage or Burger Mix. Hydrate. Better still, use 1 packet of tempeh, chopped fine, this will have a nicer flavour.*

SLICED BEEF WITH
SPRING ONIONS
GU BAK CHAR CHANG (Ref: *Mb 6*)

A spicier version of the usual Chinese dish
Preparation Time: 10 mins. Cooking Time: 6 mins
(4 persons)

INGREDIENTS

500 gm lean beef (suitable for frying) *V
5 cloves garlic
3 cm length fresh ginger
50 gms spring onions with green stalks intact
1 level dsp gr. coriander
1/2 level dsp gr. cummin
1/2 level dsp gr. black pepper
2 tbsp black bean sauce
2 tbsp rich soya sauce
1 level dsp cornflour
40 ml water
2 tbsp sesame oil
salt to taste

MAIN UTENSILS
pan or wok, skillet (if available)

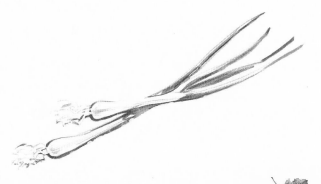

METHOD

Slice beef thinly in wide strips (2x6cm). Remove any gristles. Marinate the sliced meat with gr. coriander, gr. cummin, gr. black pepper and salt.(Remember to go easy on the salt as the black bean sauce and soya sauce are already salted.) Leave for 5 mins. while you prepare the other ingredients.

Crush or pound garlic finely. Skin ginger and cut into flat pieces and then into thin strips. Cut spring onions in approx. 3 cm length, from the green stalks to the bulbs. Discard roots. Measure out all the other ingredients and take to marshalling area. (This particular dish cooks quickly so everything must be at hand.) Now add cornflour to marinated beef and mix well to seal juices in.

Heat oil in pan/wok. As soon as oil becomes fragrant, put in garlic and ginger strips. Saute quickly. Put in beef slices and bean sauce and soya sauce. Stir rapidly. Pour in water. When meat is done, turn off heat. Then put in spring onions and give a quick stir. Remove from pan/wok and serve on skillet which had been pre-heated. Serve hot with boiled rice.

> *VEGETARIAN CONVERSION*
> *V, use either 250 gm Quorn or 1 packet of tempeh. Slice and marinate Quorn as per recipe. If using tempeh, remember that it cannot absorb the ground spices as such. Simply put excess spices into the pan/wok. If using Quorn, add veg. stock to improve taste.*

BEEF CURRY
KARI LEMBU (Ref: *Mb 7*)

Singapore-style curry with beef and potatoes
Preparation Time: 15 mins. Cooking Time: 20 mins
(4 persons)

INGREDIENTS

500 gm beef *V
1 onion, medium } *Slice and put in blender to get Mix 'A'*
3 cloves garlic
3 cm length fresh ginger
1 level tbsp hot chilli powder
2 level tbsp gr. coriander
1 level tbsp gr. cummin } *Add a few drops of water to make into a thick paste, = Mix 'B'*
1/2 level tsp gr. cinnamon
1/4 level tsp gr. cloves
1/4 level tsp gr. nutmeg
1/2 level tsp gr. turmeric
5 potatoes, medium size
4 tomatoes
5 tbsp coconut cream
2 bay leaves
500 ml water
4 tbsp veg oil
salt to taste

MAIN UTENSIL
Blender, saucepan

METHOD

Cut beef into biteable chunks. Skin and cut potatoes (halve then quarter). Cut tomatoes into wedges. Prepare Mixes 'A' and 'B' and put into separate bowls. Measure out all other ingredients and take to marshalling area.

Put Mix 'A' in saucepan over heat without oil. Stir till excess liquid is dried up, then pour in oil. Saute till slightly brown, add bay leaves and Mix 'B'. Fry till fragrant. Add meat and stir to coat it well with the spices. When surface of meat turn whitish, pour in water, add potatoes, tomatoes and salt. Allow to boil. When beef and potatoes are done, add coconut cream, turn heat down. Allow to simmer until oil separates from cream. Stir, then serve hot with boiled rice.

This recipe is the same for chicken or lamb.

> *VEGETARIAN CONVERSION*
> *V, use either 250 gm of Quorn – leave in chunks. Or 1 block firm tofu or 1 packet tempeh (cut into chunks). If using Quorn, add veg. stock to improve taste. If using tempeh, put in only at the same time as coconut cream otherwise tempeh will break up.*

FRIED MINCED BEEF WITH CELERY
(Ref: *Mb 8*)

Crunchy celery with deliciously spiced minced beef
Preparation Time: 10 mins. Cooking Time: 5 mins
(4 persons)

INGREDIENTS

250 gm minced beef *V
200 gm celery sticks (About 3 stalks with leaves)
4 cloves garlic
2 tomatoes
1 level dsp gr. cummin
1 level dsp gr. coriander
1/2 level dsp hot chilli powder
1 sprig fresh coriander
1 dsp fresh lemon juice
1 level dsp cornflour
1 tbsp light soya sauce
1 level tsp honey
60 ml water
2 tbsp sesame oil
salt to taste

MAIN UTENSIL
pan or wok with lid

METHOD

Slice diagonally across stem of celery stalks, thinly. Pound or crush garlic. Cut tomatoes into wedges. Chop up coriander finely. In a bowl, put in mince, and add gr. cummin, gr. coriander, chilli powder, cornflour and salt. Mix well. Measure out all other ingredients and take to marshalling area.

Heat sesame oil in pan/wok. When oil becomes fragrant, put in crushed garlic and saute quickly. Just as it turns brown, add in mince, water and soya sauce, taking care to stir well. Put in celery pieces and tomato wedges. Cover for 1 min.

Uncover. Check that celery is done but crunchy. Add in lemon juice and honey. Check if salt is required. Put in fresh coriander, stir, then remove from heat entirely. (For added zest, put in 1 sliced, fresh chilli too.)

> *VEGETARIAN CONVERSION*
> *V, use 250gm soya mince or Burger Mix. Hydrate, enhance with 1 dsp dried veg stock. Also quite nice with crumbled tempeh (1/2 packet). If using tempeh, don't add water immediately, allow tempeh crumble to get a bit crispy before adding water and soya sauce.*

CHICKEN IN SPICY COCONUT CREAM SAUCE
AYAM LEMAK PEKAT *(Ref: Mc 1)*

Juicy chicken simmered in a spicy cream sauce
Preparation Time: 10 mins. Cooking Time: 15 mins
(4 persons)

INGREDIENTS

500 gm boneless chicken breast *V
1 red pepper
1 onion, medium
3 cloves garlic
1 lemon grass

> *Put in blender and add a little water to get a smooth mixture = Mix 'A'*

2 level tbsp mild/hot chilli
2 level tbsp gr. cummin
1/4 level tsp gr. turmeric

> *Add a few drops of water to make into a thick paste, = Mix 'B'*

1 tsp honey
6 tbsp coconut cream
1 chicken stock *V
200 ml water
4 tbsp veg oil
salt to taste

MAIN UTENSIL
Saucepan or
wok with lid

METHOD

Cut chicken into bite pieces. Prepare Mixes 'A' and 'B' and put in separate bowls. Spoon out all other ingredients and take to marshalling area.

Put Mix 'A' in saucepan/wok without oil, over heat. Stir to get rid of excess liquid. Then pour in oil and saute mixture till brown. Add in Mix 'B' and saute till fragrant. Put in the chicken pieces and coat well with mixture. Keep on stirring until surface of chicken is cooked, pour in water and add salt, honey and stock. Cover for 2 mins. Uncover. When chicken is cooked through, pour in coconut cream. Turn heat to low. Allow to simmer until sauce thickens, stirring constantly and oil has separated from cream. Remove entirely from saucepan/wok. Serve hot with boiled rice or crusty bread.

For added zest, use 4 or 5 dried chillies, blend with Mix 'A'.

VEGETARIAN CONVERSION
*V, use 250 gm Quorn. Leave in chunks. *V, add veg, stock to improve flavour. Firm tofu is also quite nice with this recipe, use 1 block, cut into squares but reduce boiling time.

SPICY CHICKEN PIECES
AYAM GORENG *(Ref: Mc 2)*

Deliciously spiced chicken pieces, pan-fried for crispiness
Preparation Time: 5 mins. Cooking Time: 12 mins
(4 persons)

INGREDIENTS

500 gm boneless chicken breast *V
1 level tsp gr. coriander
1 level tbsp gr. cummin
1 level dsp gr. chilli
1 level tsp gr. turmeric
2 level tsp cornflour
4 tbsp veg oil
salt to taste

MAIN UTENSIL
pan or wok

METHOD

Angle the knife to slice across chicken breast so that you can get 2x6cm cm thick slices. Rub well with the gr. coriander, gr. cummin, chilli, turmeric and salt. Let it stand for 1 min. Then coat with cornflour to seal the juices in.

(Note: you can use the grill if you prefer though the chicken pieces will be crispier through frying.) Put oil in pan or wok over medium heat. Place chicken pieces individually into pan/wok. Do not overlap. When top side is cooked, turn over each piece. (Approx. 3 mins on each side.) Remove from oil when done.

Serve hot, lukewarm or cold with rice and a dish that has sauce in it. Also nice in a sandwich. Take each cooked piece and flake out with fingers and put on buttered bread, put salt and cucumber for a delicious sandwich. This recipe is just as good with turkey breast.

You can also have a European style meal with this recipe. Instead of slicing the chicken, leave in whole breasts, rub in spices and work as per recipe. Serve each breast with two vegetables.

VEGETARIAN CONVERSION
*V, 250 gm Quorn. Cut each chunk of Quorn into two so that spices can get to the centre better. Rub well with spices as per recipe. Be extra careful when frying as spices and Quorn get burned easily because they do not give out any juice(like meat does). Texture and taste is wonderful!
If using as a main course in European type meal, add another packet of Quorn. Serve with two veg.

CRISPY CHICKEN WINGS
SAYAP BAKAR *(Ref: Mc 3)*

Barbecued or Grilled chicken wings, delicately spiced
Preparation Time: 5 mins. Cooking Time: 11 mins
(2 persons)

INGREDIENTS
10 chicken wings *V
1 tsp gr. cummin
1 tsp gr, turmeric
1 1/2 tsp hot chilli powder
1 dsp sesame oil
salt to taste

MAIN UTENSIL
Baking tray, grill or barbecue

METHOD
Clean chicken wings, making sure that any feather is plucked out. With a sharp knife, slice through joint of wing without severing it so that each wing can lie flat. (Discard extreme of wing-tip if you like.)

Rub wings well with the gr. cummin, turmeric, chilli and salt. Leave aside for a few minutes while grill or barbecue is heated up. Just before grilling, pour sesame oil over wings and coat well. Lay wings out on baking tray or directly onto barbecue. 7 mins on first side and 4 on the next. Can be served hot or cold. Either eat it as a snack on its own or together with rice and a dish that has a sauce.

Note: Same recipe can be used for chicken thighs except that cooking time will be longer, 12 mins on first side, 5 on the next.

VEGETARIAN CONVERSION
*V You can use 250 gm Quorn (as per Mc 2) or 1 packet tempeh. Tempeh is a good substitute because of its crunchiness. Slice through thickness of tempeh and cut into 3cm widths. Be gentle when rubbing ground spices as tempeh is easy to break up. Grill 3 mins on first side and 2 mins on next.

CHILLI CHICKEN
SAMBAL AYAM *(Ref: Mc 4)*

A deliciously hot dish to tingle the palate
Preparation Time: 10 mins. Cooking Time: 10 mins
(4 persons)

INGREDIENTS
500 gm chicken breast fillet (boneless) *V
6 dried chillies ⎫
1 onion ⎬ *Put in blender and add a little water to get a smooth mixture = Mix 'A'*
5 cloves garlic
1 lemon grass ⎭

1 level dsp gr. cummin ⎫
1 level tsp gr. coriander ⎬ *Add water to make into a thick paste, = Mix 'B'*
1/4 level tsp gr. turmeric ⎭
1 level tsp honey
80 ml chicken stock *V
a sprig of fresh sweet basil or ordinary basil
2 mint leaves
salt to taste
4 tbsp veg oil

MAIN UTENSIL
pan/wok with lid

METHOD
Clean fillets and slice across thinly (1/2x6cm). Roughly chop up fresh basil. Prepare Mixes 'A'+'B'. Measure all other ingredients and take to marshalling area.

Put Mix 'A' in pan/wok over heat. Stir till excess liquid dries up, then add oil. Saute till slightly brown, add Mix 'B'. Put in chicken slices, mint leaves, honey, salt and stock. Stir well, then cover for 1 min. Uncover, put in chopped sweet basil, keep on stirring till sauce thickens. Remove entirely and serve hot with coconut rice/nasi lemak.

Note: If unsure about heat of dried chillies, use 2 level tbsp hot chilli powder first.

VEGETARIAN CONVERSION
*V 250 gm Quorn. Slice each chunk of Quorn. Also nice with quail eggs. 20 hard-boiled quail eggs, shell and work as per recipe. Use *V Vegetable stock instead of chicken

GRILLED CHICKEN THIGHS IN CHILLI/LEMON SAUCE
AYAM BAKAR DALAM CHILLI ASAM *(Ref: Mc 5)*

Seductively piquant sauce over crispy chicken thighs
Preparation Time: 15 mins. Cooking Time: 30 mins
(2 persons)

INGREDIENTS

Meat: 6 chicken thighs *V
1 level tsp hot chilli powder
1/2 level tsp gr. turmeric
salt to taste
1 dsp veg oil

} *Rub these into chicken thighs*

Sauce: 1 level tbsp hot chilli powder
2 tbsp black soya bean sauce
1 tsp honey
1 dsp fresh lemon juice
100 ml water

MAIN UTENSIL
Baking tray, grill, pan/wok

METHOD

After rubbing chilli and turmeric into thighs, leave aside for 5 mins. Meanwhile prepare grill and measure out all other ingredients. Add a few drops of water to the chilli powder (for the sauce) to make a paste.

Just before grilling, add oil to thighs, coat well, put under grill. 7 mins on first side, 4 mins on the next. When cooked, remove thighs from fat and pour fat and juice into pan/wok. Add chilli paste, saute till fragrant. Put in black bean sauce saute quickly. Add water, honey and lemon juice. Taste to see if you need further salt. Put in thighs and let sauce boil till it thickens. When sauce clings to thighs, remove from heat entirely and serve hot with boiled or coconut rice.

Traditionally, tamarind juice is used. If you can get it, use 2 tbsp in place of lemon juice.

VEGETARIAN CONVERSION
*V 125 gm Quorn. Use in chunks. Rub spices in well. Grill for 4 mins on first side and 2 mins on second but keep watch. Also nice with tempeh. 1/2 packet of tempeh, slice in chunks too.

SESAME CHICKEN
(Ref: Mc 6)

Tender slices of chicken stir-fried with sesame seeds
Preparation Time: 10 mins. Cooking Time: 10 mins
(4 persons)

INGREDIENTS

500 gm chicken breasts fillets *V
1 red pepper
6 cloves garlic
1 level dsp gr, cummin
1 heaped dsp gr. coriander
1 heaped tsp hot chilli powder
1 level dsp cornflour
1 heaped tbsp sesame seeds
1 dsp honey
60 ml water
salt to taste
4 tbsp sesame oil

MAIN UTENSIL
Pan/wok

METHOD

Slice across chicken breasts fillets thinly(1/2x6cm). Cut red pepper lengthwise, then slice thinly too. Pound/crush garlic. Put chicken slices in a dish and rub in gr. cummin, coriander, chilli powder, salt and cornflour. Leave aside. Measure out all other ingredients and take to marshalling area.

In a pan/wok without oil, toast sesame seeds over medium heat. Keep on stirring till seeds begin to pop. Remove and put in separate dish. Turn heat up. Pour sesame oil into pan/wok. As soon as oil is fragrant, put in garlic and red pepper. When pepper becomes limp, add chicken slices. Stir-fry till chicken changes colour then add water and honey. Taste to see if you require further salt. When chicken is done and water has dried up, tip sesame seeds back into pan, mix well. Remove entirely. Serve hot with boiled rice and a dish with salt. Try it on its own in a burger bun or sandwich.

VEGETARIAN CONVERSION
*V,1 block tofu/bean curd. Do not rub gr. cummin, coriander, chilli powder into tofu as it will break up. Instead make into paste. In a separate cup, stir cornflour into the 60 ml water. Cut tofu into 1 cm thick, rectangular pieces. After sauteing the garlic and pepper, add in spice paste, stir well. Pour in cornflour water, then add tofu pieces and follow as per recipe.

SLICE LAMB LIVER IN SOYA SAUCE
KWA CHAR *(Ref: Ml 1)*

Tender slices of liver quick-fried in soya sauce
Preparation time: 15 mins. Cooking Time: 6 mins
(2 persons)

INGREDIENTS
200 gm fresh lamb's liver (or pig's) *V
4 cloves garlic
4 cm length fresh ginger
10 gm fresh spring onions with green stalks
1 dsp gr. black pepper
2 tbsp black soya sauce
4 tbsp sesame oil

MAIN UTENSIL
Pan/wok and skillet (if available)

METHOD
Note: this dish is not nice re-heated so do not begin to cook until ready to eat. If using skillet, put in oven to heat.

Wash liver well, slice as thinly as possible (1/2x6cm). Pound/crush garlic. Cut spring onions from green stalks to bulb in 4cm length. Skin ginger and cut into strips. Measure out other ingredients and take to marshalling area. If using skillet, remove from oven and put it near stove.

Heat sesame oil in pan/wok. When fragrant, put in garlic and ginger. As soon as they turn brown, add liver slices. Stir, then add pepper and soya sauce. Stir briskly until liver changes colour and texture. Put in spring onions, stir just once then remove entirely and put into skillet to make it sizzle. Serve immediately with boiled rice.

> **VEGETARIAN CONVERSION**
> **V Use 1/2 block firm tofu. Cut into thick slices and work as per recipe.*

LAMB DRESSED IN RED
KAMBING MASAK MERAH *(Ref: Ml 2)*

Succulent lamb cooked in an appetising red sauce
Preparation Time: 15 mins. Cooking Time: 10 mins
(4 persons)

INGREDIENTS
500 gm lamb *V
4 dried chillies
1 onion
3 cloves garlic
2 cm length ginger, preferably blue ginger
1 red pepper
1 lemon grass

} *Put in blender and add a little water to get a smooth mixture = Mix 'A'*

2 level tbsp gr. coriander
1 level tbsp gr. cummin
1/4 level tsp gr. nutmeg

} *Add a few drops of water to make into a thick paste, = Mix 'B'*

70 gm tomato puree, double concentrate
150 garden peas
1 dsp honey
2 bay leaves
300 ml water
salt to taste
4 tbsp veg oil/ghee

MAIN UTENSIL
Blender, saucepan/ wok with lid

METHOD
Debone lamb if preferred. Cut into sizeable bite pieces. Prepare Mixes 'A', 'B'. Measure out all other ingredients and take to marshalling area.

Put in Mix 'A' into saucepan/wok over heat. Stir till excess liquid dries up, then add in oil. Drop bay leaves in and Mix 'B'. Saute till fragrant, then add lamb pieces until well-coated with mixture. Pour in water, add tomato puree, salt and honey. Cover for 5 mins. Uncover, turn heat to low, put in peas. When little blobs of oil appear on surface, check that meat is done, remove entirely and serve hot. Delicious with crusty bread or boiled rice.

Note: Recipe is good with any other meat too.

> **VEGETARIAN CONVERSION**
> **V 250 gm Quorn. Leave in chunks. Cook as per recipe. Might require 1 veg stock cube.*

LAMB IN MILD CURRY SAUCE
KERUMAK KAMBING *(Ref: Ml 3)*

Lamb in a green and mild sauce
Preparation Time: 15 mins. Cooking Time: 20 mins
(4 persons)

INGREDIENTS
500 gm lamb *V
1 onion
2 cloves garlic
2 cm length ginger
1 lemon grass
3 green chillies, reduce if desired
1/2 green, not red, pepper
a sprig of fresh coriander

> *Put in blender and add a little water to get a smooth mixture = Mix 'A'*

2 tbsp gr. coriander
1 tbsp gr. cummin
1 dsp gr. black pepper

> *Add a few drops of water to make into a paste, = Mix 'B'*

4 cm length cinnamon stick
3 potatoes
3 tomatoes
2 bay leaves
5 tbsp coconut cream
500 ml water
salt to taste
4 tbsp oil or veg ghee

MAIN UTENSIL
blender, saucepan with lid

METHOD
Debone lamb if preferred, if not cut into bite size pieces. After peeling tomatoes, cut each potato into 8 wedges, do the same with tomatoes. prepare Mixes 'A', 'B'. Spoon out all other ingredients and take to marshalling area.

In a saucepan over heat, put in Mix 'A' and stir to allow excess liquid to dry up. Pour in oil and saute till mixture changes colour. Drop in cinnamon stick and bay leaves. Then saute Mix 'B' till fragrant. Put in lamb pieces and potato wedges. Ensure that they are well coated with the mixture before putting in the water. Also add salt and tomatoes. Cover with lid for 5 minutes. Uncover. Check if meat and potatoes are done. Put in coconut cream. Turn heat to simmer until little blobs of oil appears. Serve hot with boiled rice or crusty bread.

Note: Recipe is also good with chicken.

VEGETARIAN CONVERSION
*V This is quite nice with just the potatoes and button mushrooms, 30 small ones. Put mushrooms in the same time as the tomatoes. Also good with Quorn, cut each chunk into two. To enhance taste, add in 1 veg stock cube or 1 dsp of dried veg stock.

GRILLED LAMB PIECES
KAMBING BAKAR *(Ref: Ml 4)*

A great recipe for the barbecue
Preparation Time: 5 mins. Cooking Time: 10 mins
(4 persons)

INGREDIENTS
500 gm boneless lamb *V
1/2 onion
2 cloves garlic
2 cm length ginger
1/4 tsp turmeric
1 dsp gr. coriander
1 dsp gr. cummin
1 dsp cornflour
1 tsp gr. black pepper

> *Put in blender and add a little water to get a smooth mixture = Mix 'A'*

1 cucumber
2 tomatoes

> *Add a few drops of water to make into a paste, = Mix 'B'*

salt to taste
1 tbsp veg oil

MAIN UTENSIL
blender, baking tray, grill or barbecue

METHOD
Slice the meat thinly but in broad pieces 1/2x4x6cm. Prepare Mix 'A' and marinate meat with this for 5 mins, (the longer the marination, the more tender the meat will be). Prepare barbecue. Spoon out all other ingredients. Run a fork down the length of the cucumber, all round, then slice across to give patterned effect. Cut tomatoes into wedges.

Add salt, cornflour and spices to meat. Coat well. When grill or barbecue is ready, add oil to meat, mix well. Then arrange meat slices in neat rows under grill or on barbecue, 6 mins on first side, 4 on next.

If using baking tray, remove meat from oil and arrange on dish with cucumber slice and tomato wedges. Nice on its own with chilli or barbecue sauce. If eating with rice, serve with another dish with sauce.

Note: Recipe is also good for beef and chicken.

VEGETARIAN CONVERSION
*V Quorn is best with this because it can accept marination with onion mixture. Use 250 gm. Slice each chunk. If barbecueing, ensure that Quorn slices are put over some kind of wire-mesh otherwise they will fall through!

GARLIC LAMB
KAMBING DALAM BAWANG PUTEH (Ref: Ml 5)

A delicious dish with garlic without the aftertaste and odour.
Preparation Time: 10 mins. Cooking Time: 12 mins
(4 persons)

INGREDIENTS
500 gm boneless lamb *V
2 onions
10 cloves garlic
1 red pepper

1 level dsp gr. black pepper   } *Add a few drops of*
1 level dsp gr. cummin   *water to make into*
                                a paste

20 ml water
2 mint leaves
3 tbsp veg ghee (or butter if preferred)
salt to taste

MAIN UTENSIL
pan/wok with lid

METHOD
Slice meat into thin, flattish slivers (1/2x4x6cm). Pound/crush garlic finely (unless you have a small blender and can blend it). Dice onions and red pepper. Chop mint leaves finely. Measure out all other ingredients and take to marshalling area.

   Heat oil (or butter) in pan/wok. Saute the garlic quickly, then put in onions and red pepper. Saute till soft but not brown. Add spice paste and saute till fragrant. Put in lamb, salt and mint, stir well. Add water and turn heat down to low, cover with lid and allow to simmer for approx 5 mins. Uncover, turn heat up again, stir continuously to avoid burning until onions turn brown and juice has been absorbed. Remove entirely from pan/wok. Serve hot with 2 veg or with boiled rice. Also nice in a crusty sandwich, cut french loaf into its length into 14 cm size and spread garlic lamb.

> *VEGETARIAN CONVERSION*
> **V. Try this with tempeh. 1 packet; cut into its thickness into thick slices. Remember that tempeh is easily broken up and has no juice to absorb so cooking time is less. Reduce water to 10 ml as tempeh is already cooked.*

PORK IN SPICY SOYA BEAN SAUCE
BABI PONGTEH (Ref: Mp 1)

A Straits Chinese New Year/Special Occasion dish
Preparation Time: 15 mins. Cooking Time: 20 mins
(4 persons)

INGREDIENTS
500 gm lean pork *V
1 onion
5 cloves garlic
3 cm length fresh ginger
2 tbsp coriander seeds
  or 4 tbsp gr. coriander
1 dsp cummin grains or 1 tbsp gr. cummin
4 fresh red chillies
2 tbsp black soya-bean sauce
2 tbsp rich soya sauce
2 tbsp fresh tamarind or lemon juice
1 dsp honey
400 ml water
4 tbsp veg oil

} *Put in blender and add a little water to get a smooth mixture = Mix 'A'*

MAIN UTENSIL
blender, pan, saucepan with lid

> *VEGETARIAN CONVERSION*
> **V. Nice with very firm beancurd, especially the type that has a 'skin' to prevent it from breaking up. Use 1 block. Cut into bite size chunks. 5 mins to simmer. Also nice with Quorn.*

METHOD
Cut pork into bite pieces. Prepare Mix 'A'. Cut into length of whole chillies without severing them. Measure out all other ingredients and take them to marshalling area.

   If using coriander seeds and cummin grains, put these into a pan without oil, over heat and dry-fry till fragrant. Turn heat off. Then blend with a little water = Mix 'B'. If not using seeds, simply dry-fry the coriander/cummin powder till fragrant, remove and then add a few drops of water to make into paste. (Flavour is greatly enhanced through using the seeds but is extra work (see I, 4).

   Put on heat again. Put Mix 'A' into saucepan and allow excess liquid to dry up by stirring. Pour in oil, saute till mixture turns slightly brown. Then add Mix 'B'. Saute till fragrant. Put in pork pieces, keep on stirring until surface of meat changes colour. Pour in water, add whole chillies, black bean sauce, soya sauce, tamarind/lemon juice and honey. (No salt is required, unless preferred, because both black bean and soya sauce are salty.) Turn heat to low, cover for 7 minutes. Uncover, check that meat is done. Serve hot with boiled rice.

   Note: Recipe is good with duck which becomes another traditional dish called Itek Sioh. Also nice with chicken.

EURASIAN CURRY
KARI SERANI (Ref: *Mp 2*)

A tangy curry unique to the Eurasians of Singapore
Preparation Time: 20 mins. Cooking Time: 20 mins
(4 persons)

INGREDIENTS
500 gm lean pork *V
4 medium size potatoes
2 tomatoes
1 onion
6 dried chillies
1 lemon grass

} *Put in blender and add a little water to get a smooth mixture = Mix 'A'*

1 level dsp gr. coriander
1 level tsp gr. cummin
a pinch of gr. cinnamon

} *Add a few drops of water to make into a paste, = Mix 'B'*

2 tbsp tamarind or lemon juice
4 tbsp coconut cream
2 lime leaves or 1 slice lemon with rind
1 tsp honey
500 ml water
salt to taste
3 tbsp veg oil

MAIN UTENSIL
blender, saucepan

METHOD
Cut pork into chunky bite pieces. Skin and cut potatoes into halves then quarters. Cut tomatoes into wedges. Prepare Mixes 'A', 'B'. Measure out all other ingredients and take to marshalling area.

Put saucepan over heat and put in Mix 'A', stir to dry up excess liquid. Then add oil and saute till mixture turns brown. Add Mix 'B' and saute till fragrant. Pour in water, add pork, potatoes, tomatoes, lime leaves or lemon slice. Add salt and honey. When potatoes are done, add tamarind/lemon juice and coconut cream. Turn down heat. When little blobs of oil appear, turn heat off and remove entirely. Serve hot with boiled rice.

> ### VEGETARIAN CONVERSION
> **V 250 gm Quorn. Leave in chunks. Cook as per recipe. To enhance flavour, add 1 veg stock cube or 1 dsp dried veg stock.*

STEAMED PORK RISSOLES
BAK EE CHWERE (Ref: *Mp 3*)

Minced pork and crab, made into rissoles then steamed
Preparation Time: 10 mins. Cooking Time: 15 mins
(3 persons)

INGREDIENTS
250 gm minced pork *V
170 gm white crab meat (or 1 can) *V
1 onion
2 cloves garlic
1 egg yolk
1 tsp gr. white pepper
1 tsp gr. cummin
1 level dsp cornflour
4 stalks spring onions
2 tsp light soya sauce
1 dsp sesame oil
salt to taste

MAIN UTENSIL
dish for steaming, steamer with lid

METHOD
Before preparing the ingredients, you can put water in steamer and put to boil.

Chop onions as fine as possible but do not mash. Pound/crush garlic. Mince crab meat. (If using canned crab meat, take out from brine.) Chop up spring onions. Put this and all other ingredients into a large mixing bowl and mix well. If it is too watery, add more cornflour. Then take one dessertspoonful of mixture each time and form into rissoles. Makes 10.

Arrange on steaming dish and put into steamer for 15 mins, cover. If steamer is not big enough to hold all the rissoles at once, cook in two lots. When cooked, rissoles should be whitish and there should be juice in the dish. Remove dish from steamer and serve rissoles hot with its juice. Particularly nice with rice porridge. If this is too foreign, eat with boiled rice.

> ### VEGETARIAN CONVERSION
> **V use 200 gm soya mince or sausage/burger mix. Hydrate. If not seasoned, add 1 dsp dried veg stock. *V, instead of crab meat, use 1/2 a small turnip; skin and chop finely. This tend to make the mixture watery so add more cornflour. Cook as per recipe. There will be less juice in the Vegetarian Conversion.*

PORK IN DRY CURRY PASTE
REMPAH BABI *(Ref: **Mp 4**)*

Another traditional Straits Chinese dish
Preparation Time: 10 mins. Cooking Time: 10 mins
(4 person)

INGREDIENTS

500 gm pork fillet *V
2 onions
3 cloves garlic
1 lemon grass

1/2 green pepper
1/2 red pepper
} *To add colour to dish, if preferred, use one type only*

3 tomatoes
1 level tbsp gr. coriander
1 level tbsp hot chilli powder
1 level dsp gr, cummin
1/4 level tsp gr. turmeric
1/4 tsp level gr. cloves
} *Add a few drops of water to make into a paste = Mix 'A'*

2 cm length cinnamon stick
2 bay leaves
a sprig of fresh coriander leaves
80 ml water
2 tbsp coconut cream
80 ml water
salt to taste
4 tbsp veg oil

MAIN UTENSIL
pan/wok

METHOD

Slice each pork fillet diagonally to get thin but broad pieces of meat(1/2x6cm). Cut tomatoes into wedges. Slice onions and peppers thinly. Pound/crush garlic. Slice lemon grass then bruise. Prepare Mix 'A'. Chop up fresh coriander roughly. measure out all other ingredients and take to marshalling area.

Heat in oil in pan/wok. Drop in cinnamon stick and bay leaves followed by bruised lemon grass, garlic, onions and peppers. Saute till onions and peppers are soft. Add spice paste and saute till fragrant. Add in pork slices and stir well to coat meat with spice mixture. Add tomatoes, water, coconut cream and salt. Stir continually to allow pork to cook and to thicken sauce. When liquid has almost dried up and sauce clings to meat, remove entirely from pan/wok. Serve hot with boiled rice or crusty bread.

VEGETARIAN CONVERSION
*V. Use 1 block beancurd. Cut beancurd into slices. (Not too fine as it will break up.) If this has no 'skin', fry beancurd in oil till it develops skin. Reduce water to 40 ml. Cook as per recipe. For a change, use Quorn. Slice Quorn.

PORK IN HOT CHILLI
SAMBAL BABI *(Ref: **Mp 5**)*

Slivers of pork in a deliciously hot sauce
Preparation Time: 10 mins. Cooking Time: 10 mins
(2 persons)

INGREDIENTS

250 gm lean pork *V
1 red pepper
6 dried red chillies
1 onion
4 cloves garlic
1 lemon grass
} *Put in blender and add a little water to get a smooth mixture = Mix 'A'*

1/4 level tsp gr. turmeric
1 tsp honey
3 tbsp coconut cream
80 ml water
salt to taste
4 tbsp oil

MAIN UTENSIL
blender, pan/wok

METHOD

Slice pork into thin slivers (1/2x6cm). Prepare Mix 'A' and add turmeric into it. Measure out all other ingredients and take to marshalling area.

Put Mix 'A' in pan/wok over heat. Stir till excess liquid dries up, then pour in oil and saute till brown. Put in pork and stir to coat well with mixture. Pour in water, add salt, honey and coconut cream. Turn heat to low till little blobs of oil appear, Remove entirely. Serve hot with boiled rice and non-spicy, light soup.

VEGETARIAN CONVERSION
*V, Try this with 1/2 packet tempeh. Cut tempeh into 6 cm length slices, lightly salt them. In a pan put 3 tbsp oil and fry the tempeh till crispy. Don't put tempeh in at the same stage as you would the pork. Pour in water which should be reduced to 40 ml. Add in salt, honey and coconut cream, let this boil a while, then put in tempeh slices. Enhance flavour if preferred, with 1/2 cube of veg stock or 1/2 dsp dried veg stock.

STEAMED SOLE
CHWERE HER *(Ref: Sf 1)*

Sole treated to a gentle Chinese seasoning then steamed
Preparation Time: 5 mins. Cooking Time: 20 mins
(2 persons)

INGREDIENTS
1 fresh lemon/dover sole *V
2 cloves garlic
4 cm length fresh ginger
1 dsp black bean sauce
1 tbsp light soya sauce
1/2 level tsp white pepper
a sprig of Chinese (or English) parsley
1 dsp sesame oil
salt to taste

MAIN UTENSIL
pan/wok, steaming dish, steamer with lid

VEGETARIAN CONVERSION
*V, Great with silken tofu. 1 block. Slice through thickness of tofu to get flattish pieces. Arrange in steaming dish. Prepare sauce and pour over as per recipe.

METHOD
If preferred, skin sole and remove head. Choose the meatier fish; pomfret is ideal for this dish. Wash fish and make three diagonal cuts on each side. Salt lightly all over and into these cuts. (Bear in mind that soya sauce is salty). Place in steaming dish.

Pound/crush garlic finely. Skin ginger and slice into long strips. Chop parsley roughly. Measure out all other ingredients and take to marshalling area. If you have two stoves, put steamer onto one and bring water to boil.

On another stove, put pan/wok over heat. Pour in sesame oil. When oil is fragrant, put in crushed garlic and ginger slices and bean sauce. When ginger turns slightly brown, pour in water, soya sauce and pepper. When the sauce boils, remove from heat and pour evenly over the fish in the steaming dish. Sprinkle chopped parsley on top and put dish in steamer. Cover and steam for approx 15 mins.

There is no necessity to turn fish over as it would be cooked through. When fish is cooked, it will turn white and give out more juice. Remove entirely and serve fish hot with its juice. Delicious with rice porridge but if this is too foreign, eat with boiled rice

GRILLED SKATE A LA SINGAPORE
IKAN PARI BAKAR *(Ref: Sf 2)*

Fresh skate, lightly spiced and grilled to perfection
Preparation Time: 5 mins. Cooking Time: 20 mins
(1 person)

INGREDIENTS
1 fresh skate *V
1/2 dsp hot chilli powder
1/4 level dsp gr. turmeric
salt to taste
2 dsp veg oil

MAIN UTENSIL
baking tray, grill or barbecue

VEGETARIAN CONVERSION
*V, Try this with 1 packet tempeh. Slice into thickness of tempeh so that you get two large pieces of tempeh which are not too thick. Very gently rub spices in. If you have tamarind juice, it gives the tempeh extra bite if you were to dip the tempeh into the juice, then barbecue or grill it.

METHOD
To clean skate properly, fill sink half-way up with warm water and use knife to clear scum. Rub chilli powder, turmeric and salt onto skate. Be fairly generous with the salt if skate is very thick in meat. Leave aside while you put on grill or barbecue. Grease a baking tray with 1 dsp oil and spoon the other over the skate. (If putting on barbecue, use a wire mesh to prevent meat from getting onto charcoal.) Put under grill for 5 mins and approx 3 mins on the other; (edge of fins will curl up when cooked).

Serve hot with chips as in a western meal or with boiled rice and a dish with sauce.

Note: This recipe is also good with mackerel, trout, sole and any meaty fish steaks like salmon, cod etc. When doing whole fish like mackerel, make three diagonal cuts on both sides of fish and make sure that spices and salt gets into them and the cavity where the gills were.

FISH IN SPICY TOMATO SAUCE
IKAN TOMATO (Ref: Sf 3)

Fresh fish steaks gently simmered in a spicy, tomato sauce
Preparation Time: 10 mins. Cooking Time: 10 mins
(3 persons)

INGREDIENTS
400 gm cod steaks (i.e 3 steaks) *V
1 onion
5 cloves garlic
4 tomatoes
1 1/2 level dsp hot chilli powder
1/2 level dsp gr. cummin
1/4 level tsp gr. turmeric
} *Add a few drops of water to make into a paste = Mix 'A'*
4 level dsp tomato puree or paste
a sprig of sweet basil (or ordinary basil)
1 tsp honey
150 ml water
3 tbsp oil
salt to taste

MAIN UTENSIL
pan/wok with lid

METHOD
Clean fish. Slice onion, pound/crush garlic finely. Cut tomatoes into wedges. Chop sweet basil roughly. Prepare Mix 'A'. Measure out all other ingredients and take to marshalling area.

Heat oil in pan/wok. Put in garlic and onion till soften. Add Mix 'A' and saute till fragrant. Then pour in water, add tomato wedges and tomato puree/paste, honey and salt. Bring to a boil. When sauce boils, put in fish, lower heat and cover for 3 mins. Uncover. Turn fish over briefly. When flesh of fish is white, it's done. Sprinkle in chopped basil and remove entirely from pan/wok. Serve hot with boiled rice.

Note: Recipe is suitable for any firm fleshed fish steaks like coley, hake etc.

VEGETARIAN CONVERSION
*V 1 block firm beancurd. Cut into squares. If bean curd has no 'skin', it might be best to put in pan over heat with oil to develop the 'skin' so that it has a crunchy taste and will not break up easily. Then drop this back into tomato sauce as per the recipe.

SINGAPORE FISH RISSOLES
OTAK OTAK (Ref: Sf 4)

A specialty of the Straits Chinese: spicy fish rissoles
Preparation Time: 15 mins. Cooking Time: 10 mins
(4 persons)

INGREDIENTS
500 gm fish fillet *V
2 onions
2 cloves garlic
1 lemon grass
3 egg yolks
1 level dsp hot chilli powder
1 level dsp gr. coriander
1 level tsp gr. cummin
1 level tsp gr. black pepper
1 level tbsp cornflour
a sprig of fresh coriander leaves
2 tbsp coconut cream
salt to taste
1 dsp sesame oil
veg oil for greasing baking tray

MAIN UTENSIL
blender, baking tray, grill

METHOD
Use any type of fresh fish fillet, preferably white rather than dark meat. Ensure that bones and skin are removed. Put in blender and mince well. Then put in mixing bowl.

Chop garlic, onions, lemon grass and fresh coriander finely in either blender or by hand – do not allow to water. Add to fish mince. Also add in all other ingredients except the oil for greasing tray. Mix thoroughly. If mixture gets too runny, then add more cornflour to reach a dropping consistency. Spoon approx 1 dessertspoonful of the mixture into your hand and shape into rissoles. Makes 15.

Put grill on. Grease tray and arrange rissoles in neat rows. Put under grill for 5 mins on first side and 4 on the next. Serve hot on its own or with boiled rice or porridge for the more adventurous.

Note: Traditionally, the fish mince is not shaped into rissoles but is wrapped in 20cm by 3cm lengths, in pandan leaves which give off a wonderful aroma when charcoal barbecued. Sometimes it is wrapped in banana leaves in 10 cm by 5 cm rectangles. Both are skewered on two ends by short wooden skewers.

VEGETARIAN CONVERSION
*V, Use 1 packet tempeh. Break it up into a fine crumble. If preferred, enhance flavour with 1 dsp dried veg stock. Also nice with soya mince or soya sausage meat.

FISH IN HOT CHILLI
SAMBAL IKAN (Ref: Sf 5)

An exciting way of serving up fish
Preparation Time: 10 mins. Cooking Time: 20 mins
(2 persons)

INGREDIENTS

2 medium size mackerel *V
4 dried chillies
1 onion
1/2 red pepper   } *Put in blender and*
4 cloves garlic   *add a little water to*
4 candle nuts or 4 whole almonds   *get a smooth mixture*
1 tsp gr. turmeric   *= Mix 'A'*
1 tbsp tamarind juice or lemon juice
1 dsp honey
60 ml water
10 tbsp oil
salt to taste

MAIN UTENSIL
blender, pan/wok with lid

VEGETARIAN CONVERSION
*V, For a change, try a combination of 1/3 packet tempeh and 1/3 block bean curd. Slice, rub gently with turmeric and salt, then fry 3 mins on first side and 2 on the second. Then work as per recipe.

METHOD

Take off heads and tails, if preferred. Make three diagonal cuts on each side of the fish. Rub gr. turmeric and salt into these cuts as well as the cavities where the gills were. In a pan/wok pour in 6 tbsp oil and put over medium heat. Put mackerels in pan/wok, approx 6 mins on each side.

While the mackerels are being fried slowly, prepare ingredients for the sauce. Prepare Mix 'A'. Measure out all other ingredients and take to marshalling area.

When fish is done, put in dish and throw away oil and clean pan/wok quickly. Turn up heat. Put in Mix 'A' and stir to allow excess liquid to dry up then add in remaining oil. Saute till mixture turns slightly brown. Pour in water and add tamarind/lemon juice, honey and salt. Gently slide the two fish back into the sauce, turn the fish to get them well coated with the sauce. Cover for 1 min. (Any uncooked part of the fish should be cooked through then.) Uncover. Stir with care in order not to break the fish up. When sauce has thickened, remove entirely. Serve hot with boiled rice.

Note: Instead of frying the fish, you can grill them but the skin will not be as crispy. Trout or fish steaks are also good with this recipe.

KING SIZE PRAWNS IN CHILLI
CHILLI UDANG (Ref: Sf 6)

Sumptuous prawns cooked to perfection in a tomato/chilli sauce
Preparation Time: 20 mins. Cooking Time: 15 mins
(4 persons)

INGREDIENTS

500 gm King Size Prawns (preferably unboiled) *V
4 dried chillies   } *Put in blender and add a*
1 onion   *little water to get a*
5 cloves   *smooth mixture = Mix 'A'*
1 level tsp cummin
2 dsp tomato puree, double concentrate
2 tsp honey
1 dsp cornflour – make into thin paste
2 egg yolks
1 egg
2 sprigs fresh coriander leaves or chinese parsley (approx 50 gm)
100 ml water
salt to taste
4 tbsp sesame oil

MAIN UTENSIL
blender, pan/wok

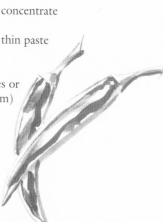

VEGETARIAN CONVERSION
*V, Nice with silken tofu, 2 blocks. Slice and fry first.

METHOD

If preferred, shell and clean prawns. (Prawns cooked in their shells give off extra flavour). To take out black vein in king-size prawn, slit spine with sharp knife, then remove vein. (Note that pink prawns have already been cooked. Depending on how long they have been boiled, their sweetness may already be dissipated. Thus, enhance flavour to dish by adding 1 stock cube. Also cut down on cooking time).

Prepare Mix 'A', then add cummin to it. Prepare cornflour. Beat egg and egg-yolks together, (too many egg-whites make the mixture runny). Chop up fresh coriander or parsley roughly. Measure out all other ingredients and take to marshalling area.

In a pan/wok over heat, put in Mix'A', stir till excess liquid is dried up. Then pour in oil, stir till fragrant. Add salt, honey, tomato puree and water. When sauce bubbles, put in prawns, keep on stirring till prawns turn pink. (If using cooked prawns, simply allow sauce to thicken). Add cornflour paste and chopped coriander/parsley. Turn off heat. Immediately add egg mixture and stir in rapidly, do not allow it to coagulate. Serve immediately with crusty bread.

Note: This cannot be reheated because egg mixture will become lumpy. If not ready to eat, don't put in egg mixture.

FISH CURRY
KARI IKAN R (Ref: Sf 7)

Fresh fish cooked in a curry with tamarind or lemon juice
Preparation Time: 10 mins.   Cooking Time: 15 mins
(4 persons)

INGREDIENTS

500 gm Huss steaks (or 4 pieces)
1 onion
1/2 red pepper
4 cloves garlic
50 gm okra i.e. lady's fingers
4 tomatoes
1 tbsp hot chilli powder   } *Add a few drops of*
1 tbsp gr. coriander   } *water to make into a*
1 dsp gr. cummin   } *paste*
1/4 tsp gr. turmeric
3 cm length cinnamon stick
1 dsp fenugreek
2 curry or bay leaves
2 tbsp coconut cream
2 tbsp tamarind or lemon juice
1 tsp honey
400 ml water
2 tbsp oil
salt to taste

MAIN UTENSIL
saucepan with lid

METHOD

Clean fish. Slice onions and pepper. Peel garlic but leave them whole. Cut tomatoes into wedges. Top and tail okra. Measure out all other ingredients and take to marshalling area.

Heat oil in saucepan. Drop in cinnamon stick, curry/bay leaves and fenugreek. Saute quickly, if it stays still, it'll burn. Put in sliced onions and pepper, saute till limp. Put in spice paste and saute till fragrant. Pour in water, add tomatoes, garlic, honey and tamarind/lemon juice. Cover quickly so that aroma will not escape. After 4 mins, uncover. Slip fish pieces in gently together with coconut cream. When fish turns white and is cooked, remove entirely from heat. Serve hot with boiled rice.

Note: Any firm white fish will be good for this recipe. Traditionally, ikan kuning, which are small fishes like mini-sole are used because they sweeten the sauce too.

VEGETARIAN CONVERSION

*V, Use 250 gm Quorn as it absorbs curry well. Cut each chunk into two. Enhance taste with 1 dsp dried veg stock or 1 stock cube. Also nice with simply the okras. Increase number of okras to approx 250 gm, for a substantial dish.

FRESH SKATE
IN LEMONY CHILLI SAUCE
IKAN PARI MASAK ASAM PEDAS (Ref: Sf 8)

Skate cooked in a unique Malay dish
Preparation Time: 10 mins. Cooking Time: 10 mins
(2 persons)

INGREDIENTS

300 gm fresh skate *V
6 dried chillies+   } *Put in blender and*
1 onion   } *add a little water to*
5 cloves garlic   } *get a smooth mixture*
4 whole candle nuts or almonds } *= Mix 'A'*
1 lemon grass
a sprig of sweet basil or ordinary
3 dsp tomato puree concentrate
2 tbsp tamarind or lemon juice
1 dsp black pepper corns
1 dsp honey
400 ml water
4 tbsp veg oil
salt to taste

MAIN UTENSIL
blender, mortar-and-pestle, saucepan with lid

VEGETARIAN CONVERSION

*V, Very nice with silken tofu, 1 block. Cut into chunks. Be aware that siken tofu is very delicate so turn heat down to medium after you have slipped the tofu pieces into the sauce. Enhance flavour of sauce with 1 dsp dried veg stock or 1 veg stock cube.

METHOD

Clean skate properly by filling sink with warmish water and use knife to clean off scum. Cut into pieces along natural lines of skate, approx 5 cm wide at the base. +(If you want a sauce with less bite, substitute with gr. chilli powder, don't put in blender but add a few drops of water to make into a paste.) Pound pepper corns. Measure out all other ingredients and take to marshalling area.

In a saucepan over heat, put in Mix 'A' and stir till excess liquid dries up. Pour in oil and saute. If using chilli powder, put in paste and saute well. Then pour in water and add tamarind/lemon juice, tomato puree, pepper corns, honey and salt. Allow to boil. Then slip skate pieces gently in together with the basil. Cover for 2 mins. Uncover, if fish has turned white and has cooked through, turn heat off and serve hot with boiled rice.

Traditionally sliced fresh chilli in dark soya sauce accompanies this dish.

Note: recipe is good for any firm fleshed fish, preferably cut into steaks.

CANNED SARDINES IN HOT CHILLI
SAMBAL SARDINE (Ref: Sf 9)

A novel and quick way to use canned sardines in tomato sauce
Preparation Time: 5 mins. Cooking Time: 5 mins
(2 persons)

INGREDIENTS

120 gm i.e. 1 can sardines in tomato sauce *V
1 onion
1 tomato
1/2 red pepper
1 level dsp hot chilli powder
1/4 level tsp turmeric
a sprig of chinese or ordinary parsley
60 ml water
1 tbsp veg oil
salt to taste

MAIN UTENSIL
pan/wok

VEGETARIAN CONVERSION
*V, Crispy tempeh is nice with this. 1/2 packet. Prep Time = 10 mins, Cooking Time: 10 mins. Tempeh should be sliced across its width approx 4 cm apart. Then saute till crispy on both sides. Use 1 tbsp tomato puree (as it hasn't got its own). Work as per recipe. If preferred, enhance flavour with 1/2 dsp dried veg stock or 1/2 veg stock cube.

METHOD

Open can of sardines and lift them out of tomato sauce. Split each sardine, remove and discard bones. Slice onion and pepper thinly. Cut tomato into small wedges. Put chill powder and turmeric into a cup to make into a paste. Chop parsley up roughly. measure out other ingredients and take to marshalling area.

Put pan/wok over heat, pour in oil. When oil is heated, put in sliced onion and pepper, saute till soft. Add in chilli paste and saute till fragrant. Pour in water and add sardines, its tomato sauce, tomato wedges, salt and chopped parsley. Stir well but do not break up sardines. When sauce bubbles, remove entirely from heat. Serve hot with boiled rice.

For extra zest, use 2 fresh chillies instead of the pepper.

CANNED SARDINE MASH
SARDINE GORENG (Ref: Sf 10)

A delicious, spicy sandwich or jacket potato filler
Preparation Time: 5 mins. Cooking Time: 5 mins
(2 persons)

INGREDIENTS

120 gm i.e 1 can sardines in tomato sauce *V
1 onion
1/2 red pepper
1 level dsp hot chilli powder
1/4 level tsp gr. turmeric
2 tbsp oil
salt to taste

MAIN UTENSIL
pan/wok

METHOD

Open can of sardines and lift them out of its tomato sauce. Split each sardine, remove and discard bones. Put sardines back into its sauce. Chop onion and pepper. Measure out all other ingredients and take to marshalling area.

Put pan/wok over heat. Pour in oil. When oil is heated, put in onion and pepper, saute till soft. Add in sardines and its sauce. Break sardines up with frying slice and add chilli powder, turmeric and salt to the mash; mix well, keep on frying till tomato sauce dries up and clings to the sardine mash. Make it slightly crispy, then remove from oil. Serve hot or luke warm in jacket potato or sandwich.

Extra bite for the adventurous if you substitute 2 fresh chillies for the pepper.

VEGETARIAN CONVERSION
*V, Great with tempeh. 1/2 packet. Use 1 dsp tomato puree (as tempeh has no sauce). It is easier to crumble tempeh with the fingers than in the pan. Put tempeh crumble in just after the onion and pepper has gone soft. Do not put in tomato sauce yet. Make sure that you fry tempeh crumble well and make it crispy before you add tomato sauce, chilli powder, turmeric and salt. Then work as per recipe.

BAKED SKATE IN COCONUT CREAM
IKAN PARI PANGGANG (Ref: Sf 11)

All the goodness of skate preserved in this lovely dish
Preparation Time: 15 mins. Cooking Time: 30 mins
(3 persons)

INGREDIENTS

3 small size skates *V
1 tbsp hot or mild chilli powder   } *Add a few drops of*
1 tbsp gr. cummin   *water to make into*
1 tsp gr. turmeric   *a thick paste*
1 lemon grass
4 heaped tbsp freshly grated/dessicated coconut
3 tbsp coconut cream
6 bay leaves
2 tbsp veg oil
salt to taste

MAIN UTENSIL
blender, aluminium foil, pan/wok, baking tray, oven

VEGETARIAN CONVERSION

*V, Firm or Extra Firm beancurd is good with this. 1 block.
Slice into thickness of beancurd to get 3 thinner but large slices.
Salt gently. As the beancurd has no inherent flavour or juice,
put 4 tbsp of water into 1 dsp of dried veg stock, mix well and
pour over beancurd slices the same time as coating them with
the coconut mixture. Be extra careful when wrapping with foil
to prevent beancurd slices from breaking up.

METHOD

Put oven on at 180 degress centigrade. To clean skates
properly, fill sink with warmish water and clean scum off
skates with a knife. Salt skates and put aside. Slice lemon
grass and put in blender together with fresh/dessicated
coconut and coconut cream. Add enough water to blend
to a smooth texture. Prepare spice paste. Cut aluminium
foil into large squares to wrap around each piece of skate,
place each skate on it.

In a pan/wok over heat, pour in the oil and saute the
spice mixture, add salt. Turn off heat. Divide this mixture
with its oil equally among the three skates. Also spoon the
coconut mixture in equal amounts over the skates.
Smooth out the combined spice and coconut mixtures
evenly on both sides till skates are well coated. Place 2 bay
leaves on each skate. Wrap each skate with the aluminuim
foil, making sure that the edges are sealed so that the juice
will not escape. Put individual skates on baking tray and
bake in oven for 30 mins. Remove from oven and foil,
taking care to scoop up the juices. Serve hot with boiled
rice or with baked potatoes.

*Note: Skate is nice because of its smooth flesh but you can
use any fish steaks. Traditionally the fish is wrapped in
squares of banana leaves which give off its flavour and
colour when baked.*

COD STEAMED WITH BLACK BEAN SAUCE
TAO CHEO HER (Ref: Sf 12)

The freshness of cod captured in this delicious sauce
Preparation time: 5 mins. Cooking Time: 20 mins
(2 persons)

INGREDIENTS

2 cod steaks approx 250 gm *V
2 cloves garlic
2 tbsp black soya bean sauce
1 tbsp light soya sauce
1 level tsp gr. black pepper
a sprig of chinese or ordinary parsley
80 ml water
1 dsp sesame oil

MAIN UTENSIL
pan/wok, steamer with lid

VEGETARIAN CONVERSION

*V, Silken tofu is best for steaming. Use 1/2 block. Cut across
to get 1 cm thick slices and arrange on dish.
Work as per recipe.

METHOD

Clean cod steaks and arrange in dish that will go into
steamer. Pound/crush garlic finely. Chop parsley. Measure
out all the other ingredients and take to marshalling area.

If you have two stoves, you can put the steamer to bring
water to the boil on one while you prepare the sauce.

Heat the sesame oil in the pan/wok. When fragrant, put
in garlic and black bean sauce, saute. Then add in water,
light soya sauce and gr. pepper. When sauce bubbles, turn
off heat. Pour sauce evenly over the cod steaks. Sprinkle the
chopped parsley too and then put dish in steamer. Cover
with lid for approx 15 mins. Uncover. Fish is white when
cooked. Serve hot with moey, the watery rice
gruel/porridge, if adventurous; otherwise just boiled rice.

*Note: Bean and soya sauce tend to be salty so the recipe does
not indicate any further salt unless preferred. For extra zest
slice two fresh chillies and saute together with garlic and bean
sauce. Traditionally white pomfret is used for this dish but
seems to be unavailable in the west. Basically a fish that has
no fiddly bones would be ideal.*

EGG CURRY
KARI TELOR *(Ref: E 1)*

Quite a nice change from the usual meat curries
Preparation Time: 5 mins. Cooking Time: 20 mins
(4 persons)

INGREDIENTS
20 quail eggs (or 8 chicken eggs) *V
3 potatoes
1 onion
2 cloves garlic
3 tomatoes
1 level tbsp hot chilli powder ⎫
2 level tbsp gr. coriander ⎪ *Add a few drops of*
1 level dsp gr. cummin ⎬ *water to make into*
1/4 level tsp gr. turmeric ⎪ *a paste*
2 cm length cinnamon stick ⎭
2 curry leaves or bay leaves
1 dsp dried veg stock or 1 veg stock cube
2 tbsp coconut cream
1 tsp honey
500 ml water
2 tbsp veg ghee
salt to taste

MAIN UTENSIL
saucepan with lid

METHOD
Put a saucepan of water to boil and put in eggs to hard-boil them. Meanwhile, skin potatoes, halve them, then quarter. Cut tomatoes into wedges. Slice onion. Bruise garlic. Prepare spice paste. Measure out all other ingredients and take to marshalling area. When eggs are ready, cool under cold tap, then shell, put aside.

If using the same saucepan as the one used for eggs, discard water and pour in veg ghee/oil. When heated, throw in curry/bay leaves, cinnamon stick, slice onions and bruised garlic. Saute till onion is soft. Put in spice paste and saute till fragrant. Then pour in water, add potatoes, tomatoes, stock, salt and honey. Cover with lid for 5 mins. Uncover, check if potatoes are done. Put in eggs and coconut cream. Allow the surface of eggs to change colour slightly as they absorb the curry. Remove entirely. Serve hot with boiled rice.

Note: For extra zest, use two fresh chillies, cut into their length but do not sever, pop into sauce the same time as tomatoes.

VEGETARIAN CONVERSION
This is already a vegetarian dish. However, for vegans, use extra firm beancurd. Cut into squares. Work as per recipe.

OMELETTE WITH MINCED BEEF
TELOR GORENG DENGAN DAGING *(Ref: E 2)*

A Singaporean type omelette with spicy mince
Preparation time: 7 mins. Cooking Time: 10 mins
(4 persons)

INGREDIENTS
5 size 1 eggs
250 gm minced beef *V
2 onions
1/2 red pepper
50 gm spring onions with green stalks
1 level tsp gr. black pepper
1 level tsp gr. cummin
1 level tsp gr. coriander
1 dsp light soya sauce
2 tbsp single cream
6 tbsp veg oil
salt to taste

MAIN UTENSIL
omelette pan/wok

METHOD
Dice onions and red pepper. Chop spring onions, set aside. Break eggs into large mixing bowl and beat well. Add minced beef, gr. black pepper, gr. cummin, gr. coriander, light soya sauce, salt and single cream. Mix thoroughly

Heat oil in omelette pan/wok. Put in diced onions and pepper. Saute till soft. Use frying slice and spread onion and pepper evenly around the pan. Stir egg mixture one more time, then pour into pan/wok evenly over the onion and pepper. When topside has set, run frying slice under omelette to detach from pan/wok. Then cut the omelette into 8 triangles and turn each one over carefully. Allow to brown on both sides. Remove from oil. Serve hot or lukewarm in a sandwich or roll or with boiled rice or moey/rice porridge or nasi lemak/coconut rice.

Note: For extra zest, substitute red pepper with 3 fresh red chillies. Slice and use in place of red pepper.

VEGETARIAN CONVERSION
*V, Use 100 gm soya mince/Burger Mix. Hydrate. Then use in place of minced beef. If already seasoned, reduce salt. Also delicious with tempeh. 1/3 packet, break tempeh into crumble and use in place of mince.

FIERY OMELETTE
TELOR GORENG DENGAN CHILLI (Ref: E 3)

Another oriental omelette, this time with crab meat
Preparation time: 10 mins. Cooking Time: 10 mins
(4 persons)

INGREDIENTS
5 size 1 eggs
1 can white crab meat *V
2 cloves garlic
1/2 small green pepper
1/2 small red pepper

} *For colour effect, so use one type if preferred*

6 button mushrooms
2 dsp hot chilli powder
2 tsp gr. black pepper
1 dsp black soya sauce
a sprig of chives
6 tbsp veg oil
salt to taste

MAIN UTENSIL
omelette pan/wok

METHOD
Pound/crush garlic finely. Dice red/green peppers. Slice button mushrooms. Chop chives. Take crab meat out from brine and squeeze out excess brine. Break eggs into a mixing bowl and beat well. Add chilli powder, gr. black pepper, soya sauce and chopped chives, salt. Mix well.

Heat oil in omelette pan/wok. Saute garlic till slightly brown. Then add red/green peppers and slice mushrooms and saute till soft. Use frying slice to spread these evenly around the pan/wok; then pour egg mixture over it. Sprinkle crab meat evenly over the mixture. When underside is cooked, use frying slice to run under the omelette to detach from pan/wok. Use frying slice to cut omelette into 8 triangles. Turn each over carefully to cook the other side. Remove from oil and serve hot or lukewarm in sandwich or roll; or with moey/rice gruel, or with nasi lemak/coconut rice or plain boiled rice.
Note: For extra zest, use 4 fresh chillies instead of the red/green peppers.

VEGETARIAN CONVERSION
*V, Try with firm tofu, 1/3 block. Dice but be careful not to make it too fine otherwise it will all break up. Saute after red/green peppers and mushrooms have turned soft very quickly to give it a 'skin' before pouring egg mixture over it. Cook as per recipe. Alternatively, increase the number of button mushrooms to 15 and work as per recipe, without tofu.

EGGS IN PEANUT SAUCE
TELOR DALAM KUAH SATAY (Ref: E 4)

A spicy crunchy peanut sauce poured over boiled eggs
Preparation Time: 15 mins. Cooking Time: 10 mins
(4 persons)

INGREDIENTS
20 quail eggs or 8 size 1 eggs
1 onion
4 cloves garlic

} *Slice and put in blender to get Mix 'A'*

11/2 level hot chilli powder
1 level dsp gr. coriander
1/2 level dsp gr. cummin
1/4 level tsp gr. turmeric
4 tbsp roasted peanuts+
3 tbsp coconut cream
1 tbsp single cream (Optional)
150 ml water
1 tsp honey
4 tbsp veg oil
salt to taste

} *Add a few drops of water to make into thick paste to get Mix 'B'*

MAIN UTENSIL
blender, saucepan with lid

VEGETARIAN CONVERSION
This is already a vegetarian dish. But for variation or Vegans, use small size new potatoes (12). Boil potatoes and arrange in dish. Pour sauce over potatoes as per recipe.

METHOD
Boil eggs in saucepan till hardboiled. (If using chicken eggs, you need to halve the eggs in order for the egg to absorb the sauce; but this tends to make the yolks drop out, so be aware.)

Meanwhile prepare Mixes 'A' and 'B'. Pound roasted peanuts but not too fine, we want the crunchy effect. Measure out all other ingredients and take to marshalling area. Cool eggs under cold tap and arrange in dish.

If using the same saucepan, discard water and put over heat without oil. Add in Mix'A'. Stir till excess liquid dries up. Then pour in oil. Saute till brown. Add in Mix'B' and saute till fragrant. Pour in water, honey and salt. (Remember to decrease salt if roasted peanuts are already salted). Bring to a boil. When sauce boils, put in roasted nuts, coconut cream and single cream. Cover immediately and turn heat down to low. (Sauce tends to spit when peanuts are in, so be careful!) After 3 mins, uncover, keep on stirring to prevent spitting and allow sauce to thicken considerably. Remove entirely from heat and pour evenly over the eggs. Serve hot with plain potato salad, just salad or boiled rice.

SCRAMBLED EGGS A LA SINGAPORE
TELOR GORENG DENGAN UDANG KECHIL (Ref: E 5)

An exotic scrambled eggs with prawns
Preparation Time: 5 mins. Cooking Time: 5 mins
(4 persons)

INGREDIENTS
5 size 1 eggs
200 gm fresh, unboiled prawns *V
2 onions
4 cloves garlic
1 level tbsp hot chilli powder
1/4 level tsp gr. black pepper } *Add a few drops of water to make into thick paste*

2 sprig of fresh coriander leaves
4 tbsp veg oil
salt to taste

MAIN UTENSIL
omelette pan/wok

VEGETARIAN CONVERSION
*V, There is no real substitute for prawns but there are many interesting alternatives. If you like commercially prepared soya sausages, use 4 and cut across each to get small pieces and use in place of prawns. Firm tofu is also quite nice. Quorn is also interesting with this.

METHOD
If using fresh, unboiled prawns, clean and shell. Chop up onions and fresh coriander separately. Pound/crush garlic finely. Break eggs into a mixing bowl and beat well, then add pepper and salt, mix thoroughly. Take all ingredients to marshalling area.

Heat oil in omelette pan/wok. When heated, put in chopped onions and garlic. Saute till onions are soft. Use frying slice to push these to the side of the pan/wok and put in chilli paste. Saute till fragrant, then put in prawns and salt, coat well with the chilli, saute till prawns turn pink. Use frying slice and take onions back to centre of pan/wok, mix well, then spread out evenly around pan/wok. Pour egg mixture over this. Allow underside to set a little before scrambling, make sure that chilli is properly mixed. Before the scrambled eggs get too cooked, put in chopped fresh coriander. (For Asian scrambled eggs, the eggs are cooked till slightly crispy). Serve hot in a sandwich or roll or even in a buttered jacket potato. Also nice with rice but accompany with a oriental soup.

EGGS IN HOT CHILLI SAUCE
SAMBAL TELOR (Ref: E 6)

Wake up the eggs with a dash of chilli
Preparation Time: 10 mins. Cooking Time: 10 mins
(4 persons)

INGREDIENTS
20 quail eggs or 8 size 1 eggs *V
1 red pepper
1 onion
6 cloves garlic } *Put in blender with a little water to get a smooth mixture = Mix 'A'*

2 level tbsp hot chilli powder
1/3 level tsp gr. turmeric } *Add a few drops of water to get Mix 'B'*

1 dsp fresh tamarind or lemon juice
1 tsp honey
80 ml veg stock
6 tbsp veg oil
salt to taste

MAIN UTENSIL
blender, saucepan, pan/wok

METHOD
Boil eggs in saucepan till hardboiled. Meanwhile prepare Mixes 'A', 'B'. When eggs are ready, cool under cold tap and shell. If using chicken eggs, halve lengthwise. Arrange on serving dish. Measure out all other ingredients and take to marshalling area.

Put pan/wok over heat, without oil. Add in Mix 'A' and stir till excess liquid dries up. Then pour in oil and saute till brown. Add Mix 'B' and saute till fragrant. Pour in stock and add lemon juice, honey and salt. Keep on stirring till sauce thickens and bubbles. Then remove entirely from pan/wok and pour over eggs. Serve hot with nasi lemak/coconut rice and slices of cucumber.

VEGETARIAN CONVERSION
For Vegans, you can use small button mushrooms in equal quantity to the quail eggs. Put mushrooms in the same time as the stock. When the sauce thickens, it should cling to the mushrooms.

SAUTEED BEANSPROUTS
TAUGEH GORENG (Ref: V 1)

Beansprouts lightly sauteed in garlic
Preparation Time: 2 mins. Cooking Time: 3 mins
(4 persons)

INGREDIENTS
300 gm beansprouts, (approx 1 packet)
2 cloves garlic
1/2 red pepper
1 dsp soya sauce seasoning
1 dsp veg oil
salt to taste

MAIN UTENSIL
deep pan/wok

METHOD
Wash beansprouts in colander, then drain. Pound/crush garlic. Slice red pepper very thinly into julienne strips.

Heat oil in pan/wok. Saute the garlic, when brown add in red pepper. Saute till soft. Put in beansprouts, salt and soya sauce seasoning. Stir-fry quickly till beansprouts turn semi-opaque. Do not let the beansprouts water as they will lose their crunchiness. Remove entirely from pan/wok. Serve hot with boiled rice and another dish.

Traditionally this dish is done with salted fish or dried prawns. If you have salted fish (1), cut into strips, fry and sprinkle on top when beansprouts are ready. If using dried prawns (6), pound and saute the same time as garlic.

> ### VEGETARIAN CONVERSION
> *This is already a vegetarian dish. However, for variation, you can use 1 slice tofu, approx 1cm thick. Cut into strips, then into 2cm lengths. Fry in oil to create a skin. Then mix in with beansprouts just as the dish is about to be ready.*

STIR-FRY MIXED VEGETABLES
SAYUR CHAMPUR (Ref: V 2)

Crunchy vegetables, stir-fried to retain their goodness
Preparation Time: 5 mins. Cooking Time: 10 mins
(4 persons)

INGREDIENTS
300 gm celery stalks (approx 4 stalks)
300 gm carrots
200 gm garden peas
2 cloves garlic
2 tbsp oyster sauce *V
1 tbsp light soya sauce
1 tsp gr. black pepper
40 ml water
2 tbsp sesame oil

MAIN UTENSIL
deep pan/wok

METHOD
Cut diagonally across celery stalks into short, thin slices. Skin carrot, then slice diagonally across to get thin, flattish slices. If using frozen peas, defrost. Pound/crush garlic finely. Measure out all other ingredients and take to marshalling area.

Heat sesame oil in pan/wok. When fragrant, put in garlic and saute till brown. Add carrots, celery and water, keep on stirring. When they are just done but still crunchy, put in peas, oyster sauce, light soya sauce, black pepper. (Test if you need salt as oyster sauce is salty). Mix well, then remove entirely and serve hot with boiled rice and another dish.

Note: Vary vegetables with baby corn, cauliflower, mange tout etc for added interest.

> ### VEGETARIAN CONVERSION
> **V, there is now a substitute for oyster sauce made with mushrooms. You can buy this in most Oriental supermarkets.*

SALAD IN PEANUT SAUCE
GADO-GADO (Ref: V 3)

A healthy salad with that extra zing
Preparation Time: 15 mins. Cooking Time: 10 mins
(4 persons)

INGREDIENTS
Salad:
4 potatoes
1 cucumber
1 onion
2 tomatoes
100 gm beansprouts
4 icebergs lettuce leaves

Sauce:
1 onion
3 cloves garlic

} *Put in blender and add a little water to get a smooth mixture = Mix 'A'*

11/2 level tbsp hot
  chilli powder
2 level tbsp gr. coriander
1/2 level tbsp gr. cummin
1/4 level tsp gr. turmeric

} *Add a few drops of water to make into a paste, = Mix 'B'*

4 tbsp roasted peanuts
3 tbsp coconut cream
1 dsp single cream
200 ml veg stock
1 tsp honey
3 tbsp veg oil
salt to taste

METHOD
Prepare salad but do not mix until ready to eat. Skin and boil potatoes, cut into wedges. Also cut onions and tomatoes into wedges. Blanch beansprouts quickly in hot, boiling water. Shred lettuce finely. Set aside.

Prepare Mixes 'A', 'B'. Pound peanuts but not too finely. Measure out all other ingredients and take to marshalling area.

Heat pan/wok without oil and put in Mix'A'. Stir till excess liquid dries up. Then pour in oil and saute till brown. Put in Mix'B', saute till fragrant. Pour in stock and add salt and honey. Bring to boil. When boiling, turn heat down slightly; add coconut cream, cream and peanuts. Stir continually till sauce thickens. Be careful as sauce tends to spit at this stage. Turn off heat. If ready to eat, mix salad and pour sauce over it.

Note; Be aware that roasted peanuts might have salt in them so reduce salt.

VEGETARIAN CONVERSION
Not required as this is purely vegetarian. If a Vegan, omit cream.

SAUTEED POTATOES
A LA SINGAPORE
UBI GORENG (Ref: V 4)

Potatoes treated to a dash of turmeric makes a tasty change
Preparation Time: 10 mins. Cooking Time: 20 mins
(4 persons)

INGREDIENTS
4 medium size potatoes
2 onions, medium size

1/2 red pepper
1/2 green pepper

} *For colour effect, so use one whole if preferred*

1 level dsp gr. turmeric
1 level tsp chilli powder
1 dsp poppy seeds
4 tbsp veg oil

MAIN UTENSIL
large pan/wok

METHOD
Skin potatoes and cut into small cubes. Dice onion and red/green peppers. Measure out all other ingredients and take to marshalling area.

Heat oil in pan/wok. Put in diced potatoes (all at once or in 2 batches depending on size of pan/wok.) When one side is cooked, turn to other side. Remove from oil. Also remove 1 tbsp of hot oil, discard. Put in poppy seeds, when they pop, put in diced onion, peppers. Saute till soft. Re-add the cooked potatoes. Sprinkle in the salt, turmeric and chilli. Mix well till potatoes are coated with the turmeric. Remove from oil. Serve hot in pitta bread satchets. Also nice with boiled rice.

Traditionally chillies instead of peppers are used. If you feel like an adventure, use 3 red chillies and 3 green chillies; slice thinly. You then omit the chilli powder.

VEGETARIAN CONVERSION
Although this is already a vegetarian dish, there is a delicious variation. Use tempeh together with the potatoes. Reduce quantity of potatoes to two and use 1/3 packet tempeh. Dice and fry tempeh like potatoes but separately; re-add to the pan/wok at the same time as the cooked potatoes.

QUICK-FRY CABBAGE
KOBIS GORENG (Ref: **V 5**)

A lovely combination of cabbage and carrots
Preparation Time: 5 mins. Cooking Time: 5 mins
(3 persons)

INGREDIENTS
400 gm white cabbage
2 carrots
3 cloves garlic
20 ml water
1 tbsp veg oil
salt to taste

MAIN UTENSIL
large pan/wok

METHOD
Wash cabbage and peel off leaves. Put a few leaves together and slice in julienne strips. Skin carrots and slice in julienne strips. Pound/crush garlic finely. Measure out all the other ingredients and take to marshalling area.

Heat oil in pan/wok. Put in garlic and saute till brown. Add in cabbage and carrot strips, salt and water. keep on stirring until cabbage turns slightly opaque. Remove entirely from pan/wok. Serve hot with boiled rice and a spicy dish.

> *VEGETARIAN CONVERSION*
> *None required as this is a vegetarian dish.*

SAVOURY PICKLED SALAD WITH SESAME SEEDS
SAYUR ACHAR (Ref: **V 6**)

Fresh vegetables blanched in a savoury pickle sauce
Preparation Time: 15 mins. Cooking Time: 5 mins
(4 persons)

INGREDIENTS
1 cucumber (approx 15cm length)
3 carrots
3 celery stalks

1/2 red pepper
1/2 green pepper
} *For colour effect, so use one whole if preferred*

1 onion, medium size

1 level dsp hot chilli powder
1/2 level tsp turmeric
} *Add a few drops of water and make into thick paste*

1 heaped tbsp sesame seeds
1 level dsp gr. almonds
2 tsp honey
290 ml malt vinegar, white
300 ml veg stock
2 tbsp sesame oil
salt to taste

MAIN UTENSIL
large pan/wok with lid, (3 air-tight storage jars)

METHOD
Cut across cucumber into 5 cm lengths. Halve and remove soft pulp. Then cut into 1/2 cm thickness strips. Skin carrots, then cut into 5 cm lengths, halve then cut into 1/2cm thickness strips. Do the same for the celery stalks. Prepare spice paste. Measure out all the other ingredients and take to marshalling area.

Put pan/wok over heat without oil. Put in sesame seeds and toast until they 'pop' or 'jump'. Stir continuously to prevent burning. Remove and set aside. Pour in sesame oil. When fragrant, saute spice paste. Then add gr. almonds. Mix well. Then pour in vinegar and water, also add salt and honey. Cover and allow to boil for 2 mins. Uncover. Blanch vegetables quickly in vinegrette and remove vegetables from it. Turn heat off and allow vinegrette to cool. When vinegrette is completely cool, put vegetables back in and add toasted sesame seeds. Mix well, then serve with boiled rice or store in airtight jars in refrigerator and serve as required.

> *VEGETARIAN CONVERSION*
> *None required as this is purely vegetarian.*

LENTILS WITH MIXED VEGETABLES
SAYUR DAL (Ref: V 7)

All the goodness of vegetables enhanced with nutritious lentils
Preparation Time: Inclusive of cooking time as vegetables are prepared while lentils are being boiled.
Cooking Time: 30 mins

INGREDIENTS
50 gm red lentils
1 onion, large
3 cloves garlic
1 dsp gr. coriander
1 dsp gr. cummin
1 tsp gr. black pepper
4 potatoes
75 gm cauliflower
100 gm peas
1 brinjal/egg plant
10 cherry tomatoes
200 ml veg stock
600 ml water (for boiling lentils)
2 tbsp coconut cream
1 dsp fresh lemon juice
3 bay leaves
1 tbsp oil
salt to taste

} *Add a few drops of water to make into a thick paste*

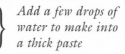

MAIN UTENSIL
saucepan with lid,
small pan

METHOD
Wash lentils till water is clear. Then put to boil with 600 ml water, (keep on scooping out froth otherwise it makes you gaseous). Boil for approx 15 mins or until lentils are soft.

Meanwhile prepare vegetables. Dice onion. Pound/crush garlic. Skin and cut potatoes into wedges. Cut cauliflower into florets. Dice the brinjal/egg plant into bitesize cubes. If using frozen peas, defrost. Prepare spice paste. Measure out all the other ingredients and take to marshalling area.

When lentils are soft, put in potatoes, veg stock and salt. When potatoes are half done, put in cauliflower florets, brinjals, tomatoes and bay leaves. On a separate hob, heat oil in a pan and saute onion and garlic. Then add the spice paste, saute till fragrant. Then scoop out with oil and put into lentil mixture. Add the coconut cream and lemon juice. Turn heat down slightly to allow sauce to thicken. Remove entirely and serve hot with boiled rice.

Note: Recipe also good as a soup. Dice vegetables into chunky pieces. Increase volume of stock to 600 ml.

VEGETARIAN CONVERSION
Not required. For variation, cut 1/2 block extra firm tofu, into bite-size cubes and put in sauce/soup.

BROCCOLI WITH OYSTER SAUCE
(Ref: V 8)

Fresh broccoli gently braised with oyster sauce
Preparation Time: 5 mins. Cooking Time: 5 mins
(3 persons)

INGREDIENTS
400 gm broccoli
2 cloves garlic
2 tbsp oyster sauce *V
1 tbsp light soya sauce
40 ml water
1 dsp sesame oil

MAIN UTENSIL
large pan/wok

METHOD
Separate broccoli florets from the stems. Slice diagonally across stems to get thin, flattish pieces. Pound/crush garlic. Measure out all other ingredients and take to marshalling area.

Heat oil in pan/wok. When fragrant, put in garlic and saute till brown. Put in broccoli stems and fry until they just change colour. Put in florets together with water, oyster sauce and light soya sauce. Stir continuously, turning broccoli over rapidly. When stems are translucent, broccoli will be nicely done but crunchy. Serve hot with boiled rice or moey/rice porridge.

Note: No salt is required, unless preferred, because both the oyster and light soya sauce are salty. This recipe is also good for most leafy vegetables like chinese leaves, savoy cabbage.

VEGETARIAN CONVERSION
*V, There is now a substitute for oyster sauce made with mushrooms. You can buy this at an oriental supermarket.

LEEKS WITH WALNUTS IN BEAN SAUCE
(Ref: V 9)

Leeks with a nutty difference
Preparation Time: 5 mins. Cooking Time: 5 mins
(3 persons)

INGREDIENTS
400 gm leeks
1/2 red pepper
2 cloves garlic
50 gm walnut halves
1 tbsp yellow bean sauce
3 tbsp water
1 tbsp veg oil

MAIN UTENSIL
large pan/wok

METHOD
Clean leeks thoroughly, slice across stem diagonally in 5cm lengths. Pound/crush garlic finely. Slice red pepper thinly. Measure out all other ingredients and take to marshalling area.

Heat oil in pan/wok. Put in garlic and saute till brown. Add sliced red pepper and saute till soft. Put in leeks, bean sauce, walnuts and water. Keep on stirring until leeks are wilted but still crunchy. Remove entirely from pan/wok. Serve hot with boiled rice or moey/rice porridge.

Note: Salt is not required unless preferred as bean sauce tend to be salty. For extra bite, you can use 2 red chillies instead of the pepper.

> *VEGETARIAN CONVERSION*
> *Not required.*

MANGE TOUT PEAS WITH CASHEW NUTS
(Ref: V 10)

Fresh mange tout with that extra crunch
Preparation Time: 5 mins. Cooking Time: 10 mins
(3 persons)

INGREDIENTS
400 gm mange tout peas
100 gm cashew nuts (unroasted)
3 cloves garlic
1 tbsp soya sauce seasoning
1 tbsp sesame oil
salt to taste

MAIN UTENSIL
large pan/wok

METHOD
Top and tail the mange tout peas, string if necessary. Pound/crush garlic finely. Measure out all the other ingredients and take to marshalling area.

Heat oil in pan/wok. When fragrant, put cashew nuts in and fry quickly, making sure they do not burn. When nicely brown, remove from oil. Saute garlic till brown. Put in mange tout, soya sauce and salt. Re-add the cashew nuts. Keep on stirring till mange tout becomes slightly translucent. Remove entirely. Serve hot with boiled rice and a spicy dish.

Note: You can also use ready roasted cashews. If salted, reduce salt.

> *VEGETARIAN CONVERSION*
> *Not required.*

OKRA/LADY'S FINGERS IN TURMERIC
(Ref: V 11)

A touch of turmeric to okra and fresh coconut for added zest
Preparation Time: 10 mins. Cooking Time: 10 mins
(3 persons)

INGREDIENTS
350 gm okra/lady's fingers
1/2 onion
2 cloves garlic
1/2 red pepper
1 tomato
1 tsp chilli powder
1 tsp gr. turmeric
1 tbsp freshly grated/dessicated coconut
1 dsp poppy seeds
4 tbsp water
1 tbsp veg oil
salt to taste

MAIN UTENSIL
large pan/wok

METHOD
Top and tail okra. Slice across diagonally in 2.5 cm length. Cut tomato into small wedges. Slice onion and red pepper thinly. Pound/crush garlic finely. Measure out all the other ingredients and take to marshalling area.

Heat oil in pan/wok. Put in poppy seeds and garlic, saute till garlic turns brown. Then put in sliced onion and pepper, saute till soft. Add in okra and tomato together with water and salt. Stir continuously until okra is cooked through. Make sure that water dries up completely. Then sprinkle in the chilli powder, gr. turmeric and coconut. Fry well so that coconut is coloured. Remove from oil. Serve hot with boiled rice. Also nice in a jacket potato or pitta bread sachet.

> *VEGETARIAN CONVERSION*
> *Not required.*

CAULIFLOWER FLORETS IN SESAME
(Ref: V 12)

A delightful way of serving up cauliflower
Preparation Time: 5 mins. Cooking Time: 10 mins
(3 Persons)

INGREDIENTS
250 gm cauliflower
200 gm baby corn
2 carrots
3 cloves garlic
1 tsp gr. black pepper
1 tbsp sesame seeds
4 tbsp water
1 tbsp sesame oil
salt to taste

MAIN UTENSIL
large pan/wok

METHOD
Cut cauliflower into small florets. Top and tail baby corn and cut into strips lengthwise. Cut across carrots into 6cm lengths and slice thinly into julienne strips. Pound/crush garlic finely. Measure out all the other ingredients and take to marshalling area.

In pan/wok without oil, toast sesame seeds till they pop. Remove and set aside. Pour oil into pan/wok. When fragrant, saute garlic till brown. Put in carrots, cauliflower and water. Stir continuously till vegetables are cooked halfway. Add salt and pepper. Then put in baby corn, stir till water dries up. Then re-add sesame seeds, stir till vegetables are well-coated with sesame, then remove entirely. Serve hot with a dish that has a sauce.

> *VEGETARIAN CONVERSION*
> *Not required.*

SAVORY LAMB SOUP
SUP KAMBING *(Ref: Sp 1)*

An extremely popular exotic soup
Preparation Time: 10 mins. Cooking Time: 15 mins
(4 persons)

INGREDIENTS

500 gm lamb, boneless *V
1 onion
2 cloves garlic
1 lemon grass
2 cm length ginger
2 tbsp gr. coriander
1 tbsp gr. cummin
a pinch of gr. cinnamon
a pinch of gr. cloves
a pinch of star anise
1 tbsp gr. almonds
1 lamb stock cube *V
2 tbsp coconut cream
4 cm length cinnamon stick
2 mint leaves
a sprig of fresh coriander leaves
5 shallots (for garnishing)
600 ml water
4 tbsp veg ghee
salt to taste

MAIN UTENSIL
blender, saucepan with lid

Put in blender and add a little water to get a smooth mixture = Mix 'A'

Add a few drops of water to make into a paste, = Mix 'B'

METHOD

Dice lamb into small cubes. Slice shallots. Chop up fresh coriander. Prepare Mixes 'A', 'B'. Measure out all other ingredients and take to marshalling area.

Heat ghee in saucepan. Saute shallots till brown, remove from oil and set aside for garnishing. In the same oil, put in Mix 'A', stir till excess liquid dries up. (If necessary, add a little more oil). Saute till brown. Then put in cinnamon stick and Mix 'B', saute till fragrant. Put in lamb cubes and stir till they are well coated with the spices. Pour in water and put in stock cube, salt and mint leaves. Cover. Allow to boil for 2 mins. Uncover. Put in gr. almonds and coconut cream. Turn down heat to simmer until lamb is completely cooked. Before serving, garnish with chopped coriander and sauteed onions. Serve piping hot with crusty bread.

Note: This is one of the rare Asian soups which is in itself a meal.

> **VEGETARIAN CONVERSION**
> **V, very authentic with Quorn! Use 250 gm and cube as per recipe. *V, Use veg stock instead of meat.*

CLEAR POTATO/PORK SOUP
BAK TNG *(Ref: Sp 2)*

A thin, clear soup that complements spicy dishes
Preparation time: 5 mins. cooking Time: 15 mins
(2 persons)

INGREDIENTS

200 gm pork, slightly fatty *V
4 potatoes
1 onion
200 gm or 1 can button mushrooms in brine
1 tbsp light soya sauce
3 cm length cinnamon stick
2 pieces cloves
500 ml meat stock *V
1 tsp gr. white pepper
salt to taste

MAIN UTENSIL
saucepan with lid

METHOD

(As there's no fat used for this soup, slightly fatty pork gives off its own.) Cut pork into bite size pieces. Cut potatoes into small wedges and do the same for the onion. Take mushrooms out from the can. (Canned mushrooms in brine gives off a certain flavour to the soup.)

Put all the ingredients into a saucepan and put over heat. Bring to the boil, cover with lid for 5 mins. Uncover. Cook till potatoes and pork are well cooked. Serve hot with rice and a spicy dish.

> **VEGETARIAN CONVERSION**
> **V, Use 1 block Silken Tofu. Cut into bite size pieces but do not put in until potatoes are almost done, otherwise Tofu will break up. *V, Use veg stock. Also add 1 tbsp sesame oil as there is no fat in tofu.*

CORIANDER CHICKEN SOUP
SUP AYAM *(Ref: Sp 3)*

Shredded chicken in a coriander soup
Preparation Time: 5 mins. Cooking Time: 10 mins
(2 persons)

INGREDIENTS
2 boneless chicken fillets *V
4 shallots
3 cloves garlic
1 level dsp gr. coriander
1 heaped tsp gr. cummin
1 level tsp gr. black pepper
a sprig of fresh coriander leaves
2 pieces cloves
2 bay leaves
500 ml chicken stock *V
1 tbsp sesame oil
salt to taste

} *Add a little water and make into a thick paste*

MAIN UTENSIL
saucepan with lid

METHOD
Clean chicken fillets but leave them whole. Slice shallots. Pound/crush garlic finely. Chop coriander leaves. Prepare spice paste. Measure out all other ingredients and take to marshalling area.

Heat oil in saucepan. When fragrant, put in cloves and garlic and shallots. Saute till shallots turn brown. Put in spice paste and saute till fragrant. Pour in stock, add salt, bay leaves and allow to boil. Then put in whole fillets. Cover for 5 mins. Turn heat down and remove chicken from the soup. Cool chicken under cold tap and tear chicken into shreds with fingers. (If you use a knife, the shreds are not so fine). Return chicken to soup, turn heat up. Put in chopped coriander. Serve hot with boiled rice.

> *VEGETARIAN CONVERSION*
> *V, Use 150 gm Quorn. Slice each chunk very thinly in julienne strips.(It's too tedious to shred Quorn by hand). Therefore it's not necessary to remove it from soup. *V, Use veg stock.*

FISH SOUP
SUP IKAN *(Ref: Sp 4)*

Fresh, delicate fish in a light tomato soup
Preparation Time: 7 mins. Cooking Time: 10 mins
(2 persons)

INGREDIENTS
300 gm cod fillet *V
1/2 onion
1/2 red pepper
3 cloves garlic
6 cherry tomatoes
1 level dsp gr. cummin
a pinch of gr. nutmeg
1 tsp gr. black pepper
2 tbsp tomato puree concentrate
1 fish stock cube
a sprig of fresh dill
500 ml water
1 dsp sesame oil
salt to taste

} *Add a little water and make into a thick paste*

MAIN UTENSIL
saucepan

METHOD
Take off skin of fillets very gently. Remove all bones carefully. Dice fish fillets in 1.5cm chunks. Dice onion and red pepper. Chop up the fresh dill. Prepare spice paste. Measure out all other ingredients and take to marshalling area.

Heat oil in saucepan. When fragrant, put in garlic, onion and pepper. Saute till onion and pepper turn soft. Put in spice paste and saute till fragrant. Pour in water and add tomato puree, salt and stock. Allow to boil. When water is boiling, gently slide in diced fish and dill. As soon as the fish turn white, turn off heat. Serve hot with boiled rice or on its own with crusty bread.
Note: To make it into a full meal, add cooked 25 gm macaroni pasta shells.

> *VEGETARIAN CONVERSION*
> *V, Try this with Extra Firm beancurd, 1/2 block. Dice into 1.5cm squares. Work as per recipe. *V, Use veg stock cube.*

CRAB/PORK BALL SOUP
HOY BAK TNG *(Ref: Sp 5)*

Balls of crabmeat and minced pork in a delicious soup
Preparation Time: 20 mins. Cooking Time: 10 mins
(3 persons)

INGREDIENTS

250 gm minced pork *V
170 gm/1 can white crab meat *V
100 gm or 2/3 can bamboo shoots
1 onion
4 cloves garlic
1/2 red pepper
3 egg yolks
1 level tsp gr. cummin
1 level tsp gr. black pepper
1 level tbsp cornflour
2 sprigs fresh coriander leaves
500 ml meat stock *V
2 dsp sesame oil
salt to taste

MAIN UTENSIL
blender/chopper, saucepan with lid

METHOD

Take crab meat out from brine and chop finely. Use blender/chopper to chop onion and red pepper finely but not to a mushy state. Pound/crush garlic. Slice bamboo shoots in short, thin strips. Chop fresh coriander leaves.

In a large mixing bowl, put minced pork, crab meat, onion, red pepper, sliced bamboo strips, egg yolks, cummin, black pepper, cornflour, salt and 1 dsp sesame oil. Mix well. Take one dessertspoonful of mixture and shape into balls. (If too watery, add more cornflour.) Makes 15. Measure out meat stock and take to marshalling area.

Heat the other 1 dsp sesame oil in saucepan. Put garlic in and saute till brown. Pour in stock, (and add salt if preferred). Allow to boil. When boiling, gently slide in the minced balls. Cover for 2 mins. Uncover, when meat balls have turned white, cook for another 2 mins. Remove entirely, garnish with chopped coriander. Serve hot with boiled rice.

Traditionally slices of abalone are put into the soup as well. As abalone is an expensive delicacy, this soup is usually served on special occasions like Chinese New Year.

VEGETARIAN CONVERSION
*V, Use 70 gm SosMix. Hydrate. *V,Instead of crab meat, use 2 water chestnuts. Grate water chestnuts finely and use in place of crab meat. *V, Use veg stock. Reduce egg yolks to 2 because soya mince does not hold as well as meat mince and will disintegrate in the soup.

PORK SATAY
SATAY BABI *(Ref: Cs 1)*

Slivers of pork, spiced, skewered and barbecued
Preparation Time: 30 mins. Cooking Time: 20 mins
(4 persons)

INGREDIENTS

300 gm boneless pork *V
1 onion
6 cloves garlic
2 cm length ginger
1 lemon grass

} *Put in blender and add a little water to get a smooth mixture = Mix 'A'*

2 level tbsp gr. coriander
1 Level tbsp gr. cummin
1 tbsp chilli powder
1 tsp gr. turmeric
a pinch of cinnamon

} *Add a few drops of water to make into a thick paste, = Mix 'B'*

8 tbsp roasted peanuts
5 tbsp coconut cream
1 tbsp single cream
400 ml veg stock
1 dsp honey
4 tbsp veg oil
salt to taste

MAIN UTENSIL

blender, saucepan with lid, 28 skewers, approx 14cm length (preferably wooden), grill or barbecue

METHOD

Slice pork in thin flattish pieces approx 1/2x2x7cm. Prepare Mixes 'A','B'. Pound/grind peanuts but not too fine. Measure out all the other ingredients and take to marshalling area.

Take 1 dsp of Mix'A' and 1 dsp of Mix'B', add salt and put on pork slices. Mix well until pork slices are thoroughly coated. Leave aside. Also spoon out 1 dsp oil for use later.

Sauce: Put the rest of Mix'A' without oil in the saucepan over heat. Stir till excess liquid dries up, then pour in oil. Saute till brown. Put in rest of Mix'B' and saute till fragrant. Pour in stock, add coconut cream, salt and honey. When boiling, put in roasted peanuts and cream. Cover for 3 mins as peanuts cause spitting. Uncover, stir well till sauce thickens. Turn off heat and use when satay is ready.

Satay: Take each slice of marinated pork and skewer it in such a way that it produces a ridged effect. (Leaving it flat makes it hard). On the average, 2 slivers of meat will make a 7cm satay. Makes approx 28 satay. Use a pastry brush or rolled kitchen towel to dip in the remaining oil and brush satay lightly. Then put satay over charcoal flame or grill. (If using wooden skewers, ensure that exposed parts of skewers are wrapped in foil if under grill. On barbecue, make sure that skewers are not directly over flame.) 5 mins on each side. Serve hot with sauce.

Traditionally, satay and its sauce is accompanied by a salad made up of fresh cucumber and raw onions cut into small wedges together with ketupat. The latter is a compressed rice cake made by boiling rice in a weaved coconut-leaved bag approx 6cm x 3cm x 6cm. The coconut-leaves give the rice its colouring and flavour. A home-alternative is to boil rice with salt till extremely soft, drain the water and put in a dish. Place a muslin cloth over the dish, then put something heavy to compress the rice. Put overnight in a fridge. When compressed rice cake has set, cut into small squares. This is only tasty when dipped in the peanut sauce.

To serve satay, put hot sauce in little bowls with several sticks of satay on a plate together with the ketupat and salad. After sliding off a piece of meat with the teeth, the stick is reused to pick the pieces of ketupat, cucumber or onion. Delicious with chicken or beef too.

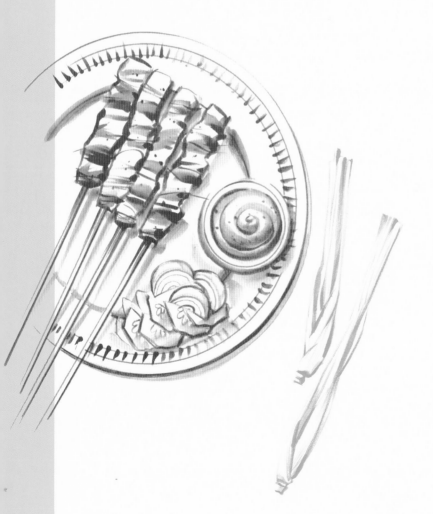

VEGETARIAN CONVERSION

V, Use 250 Quorn. Slice Quorn very thinly but leave enough width so that skewer can pierce into it. Marinate as per recipe. As Quorn is not very elastic, it will not be possible to create a ridged effect. You will have to make do with 3 or 4 pieces of Quorn on one skewer. It is still as delicious though.

PLAIN CREPE
ROTI JALA (Ref: CS 2)

A very light crepe ideal for most spicy dishes
Preparation Time: 5 mins. Cooking Time: 20 mins
(2 persons)

INGREDIENTS
200 gm ordinary flour
4 eggs
4 tbsp coconut cream
400 ml milk
1 tsp gr. black pepper
1 drop natural food colouring, yellow (Optional)
salt to taste
2 tbsp oil

MAIN UTENSIL
mixing bowl, crepe pan or griddle

CAUTION!
NOT GLUTEN-FREE

VEGETARIAN CONVERSION
Not required.

METHOD
In a mixing bowl, sieve in flour and salt. Pour in milk and get rid of any lumps that result. Then put in coconut cream, break in eggs, add pepper and food colouring if required. Stir well with wooden spoon till mixture is smooth.

Heat pan or griddle. Grease very lightly. Take 1/3 a cup of batter and pour into pan/griddle. Tilt pan till batter runs smoothly round it. (If using griddle use back of ladle to smooth the batter.) When top side of crepe is cooked, turn over with a frying slice. As soon as sides curl up slightly, remove. When the next one is on the pan, fold the cooked one into a triangle. Serve hot or luke warm.

Traditionally this is eaten with Keema i.e.Mb 1; however any spicy dish with a sauce is just as good. Traditionally a 3-pronged mould is used for making this crepe. The batter flows out of the three prongs and runs onto the pan/griddle creating a lacy network. Hence the crepe is called Roti Jala i.e. Net Bread/Crepe. Because of the lacy effect, two crepes are folded back-to-back together to make it more substantial.

PORK RIBS IN SPICY BEAN SAUCE
PAI KWAT (Ref: Cs 3)

Just a light snack cooked in a delicious bean sauce
Preparation time: 5 mins. Cooking Time: 10 mins
(2 persons)

INGREDIENTS
600 gm pork ribs, i.e. 12 ribs, *V
4 cloves garlic

1 level tbsp mild chilli powder } *Add a few drops of water to make into a thick paste*
1 level tbsp ground coriander

1 level tsp gr. black pepper
2 level tbsp black bean sauce
1 tbsp rich soya sauce
100 ml water
1 tbsp sesame oil

MAIN UTENSIL
pan/wok with lid

METHOD
Clean ribs and sever if attached to make individual ribs. Pound/crush garlic finely. Prepare spice paste. Measure out all other ingredients and take to marshalling area.

Heat oil in pan/wok. When fragrant, drop in garlic and saute till brown. then put in spice paste and saute till fragrant. Put in ribs and stir to coat them with the spice paste. When the ribs change colour a little, put in black bean sauce and rich soya sauce and water. Cover for 4 mins. Uncover. Stir well and allow sauce to thicken and cling to the ribs. Serve hot. Use crusty roll to sop up sauce.

Note: You can also brown the cooked ribs under the grill for extra flavour. Put cooked ribs in a dish that can go under the grill, for 4 mins. Don't let the sauce dry up completely.

VEGETARIAN CONVERSION
*There is no real substitute for pork ribs. But you can get a similar taste with Quorn. Use 100 gm *V. Cut each piece of quorn into two. With Quorn it's nicer to brown it, so put in a dish and place under grill for 3 mins. Also nice with Extra Firm Tofu, 1/2 block, but be very gentle when cooking.*

SPICY SPRING ROLLS
POPIA GORENG *(Ref: Cs 4)*

Easy to make springs rolls deep fried for extra crispiness
Prepartion Time: 25 mins. Cooking Time: 20 mins (or 5 mins per lot)
(4 persons)

INGREDIENTS
500 gm minced pork *V
170 gm (i.e. 1 can) white crab meat *V
2 onions
1 carrot
1 dsp meat seasoning *V
1 tsp gr. coriander
1 dsp gr. cummin
1 tsp gr. black pepper
3 egg yolks
1 dsp light soya sauce
1 dsp sesame oil
2 dsp cornflour
16 small spring roll sheets
1 oz of watery cornflour paste (for sealing edges)
deep fat for frying

MAIN UTENSIL
chip-fryer/wok

CAUTION –
NOT GLUTEN FREE

METHOD
Take crab meat out from brine and mince. Chop onions finely. Grate carrot finely too. In a large mixing bowl, add minced pork, crab meat, onion, carrot. seasoning, spices, egg yolks, cornflour, sesame oil, light soya sauce and salt. Mix thoroughly. (To taste if you have enough salt, make a small ball of mixture and fry, then taste).

Before rolling, heat fat in deep fryer/wok.

If using large sheets, cut into 12 cm square. Take 1 dessertspoonful of mixture and put onto each sheet. Roll once over, turn in both ends and roll till end of sheet. Seal edge with cornflour paste. Makes 16. Fry till golden brown, approx 5 mins. Serve hot with tomato/chilli sauce combination.

VEGETARIAN CONVERSION
V Use 250 gm minced Quorn in place of the mince. Use 1 small mouli, approx 12 cm (or 1/2 small turnip) in place of crabmeat. Grate this finely. Use 1 dsp veg stock as seasoning. Work as per recipe.

FISH RICE PORRIDGE
HER MOEY *(Ref: Cs 5)*

A very nourishing and complete meal
Preparation Time: 5 mins. Cooking Time: 20 mins
(1 person)

INGREDIENTS
50 gm pudding rice
100 gm fresh cod fillet *V
1 egg
4 cm length fresh ginger
1 fish stock cube *V
1 tsp gr. black pepper
1 dsp light soya sauce
a sprig of chives
600 ml water
salt to taste
1 dsp sesame oil

MAIN UTENSIL
saucepan

METHOD
Clean rice well till water is clear. Place in saucepan and boil till extremely soft and broken.

Meanwhile, clean fish fillet and ensure that all bones are taken out. Then dice fish into cubes. Also dice ginger finely. Chop chives. Measure out all ingredients and take to marshalling area.

When porridge is well cooked, put in stock, ginger and gr. pepper. Allow to boil. Then put in fish cubes and stir gently so that they do not break up. Add sesame oil, light soya sauce and chives. Stir until fish is cooked. Take off heat. If ready to eat, break an egg into it and stir quickly. Serve piping hot.

Note: If preferred, omit egg. Fish can be substituted with any meat, minced or sliced finely. If using meat, use meat stock.

VEGETARIAN CONVERSION
V, Use 1/3 block Silken Tofu. Cut into cubes. Use 1 veg stock cube in place of fish stock. Cook as per recipe. If you can find braised tofu, it is much tastier. Use 100 gm, take out from sauce and cut into cube. Omit the 1 dsp light soya sauce as in the recipe, and use 1 dsp of the braised liquid instead.

SINGAPOREAN FRIED RICE
NASI GORENG (Ref: Cs 6)

Savoury rice with a pot-pourri of spam and vegetables
Preparation Time: 20 mins.   cooking Time: 20 mins
(4 persons)

INGREDIENTS
200 gm boiled rice+
250 gm spam+
3 cloves garlic
1 red pepper
1 carrot+
100 gm french beans+
2 celery stalks+
100 gm sweet corn+
150 gm peas +
5 spring onion stalks
1 dsp hot chilli powder
1 tbsp gr. coriander
1 dsp gr. cummin
1 tbsp light soya sauce
4 eggs
salt to taste
6 tbsp oil

MAIN UTENSIL
Large frying pan/wok

METHOD
Dice spam into cubes. Pound/garlic finely. Dice peppers, carrot. Top and tail french beans and cut across in small pieces, do the same with celery. Defrost peas and sweet corn if frozen. Prepare spice paste. Break eggs into a bowl and put in a little salt, beat well. Measure out all other ingredients and take to marshalling area.

Heat 4 tbsp of oil in the pan/wok. Pour in beaten egg. Just as the underside of the egg mixture gets cooked, sprinkle the rice evenly all over. Use the frying slice and stir fry well till rice is well coated and egg is slightly brown. Remove from pan/wok.

Heat remaining 2 tbsp oil in the same pan/wok. Put in garlic and peppers. Saute till peppers are soft. Then add spice paste and saute till fragrant. Put in the spam, carrot, celery, and french beans. Add soya sauce and a little salt, saute quickly. Don't over cook, let the vegetables remain crunchy. Put in sweet corn and peas. Stir till all liquid is dried up, then re-add fried egg rice. Mix thoroughly. Add chopped chives and remove entirely. Serve hot.

Note: +Marks all ingredients that can be used from leftovers. Use any meat in place of spam and any vegetables.

> **VEGETARIAN CONVERSION**
> *Simply omit meat. If preferred, put in leftover Tofu or tempeh. Cut into cubes.*

SINGAPOREAN FRIED NOODLES
BEE HOON GORENG (Ref: Cs 7)

Vermicelli fried the Singaporean way
Preparation Time: 20 mins. Cooking Time: 15 mins
(4 persons)

INGREDIENTS
250 gm vermicelli
250 gm lamb+, *V
1 onion
4 cloves garlic
3 potatoes+
3 tomatoes
50 gm baby corn
100 gm mange touts
70 gm button mushrooms+
250 gm beansprouts
1 tbsp hot chilli powder
1 tbsp gr. coriander
1 dsp gr. cummin
4 eggs
2 tbsp tomato ketchup
2 tbsp rich soya sauce
a sprig of coriander
6 tbsp veg oil
salt to taste

} *Add a few drops of water to make into a thick paste*

MAIN UTENSIL
Large pan/wok

> *VEGETARIAN CONVERSION :*
> *Omit meat.*

METHOD
Put vermicelli in a large bowl and pour hot, boiling water over it. Leave for 4 mins, then drain through sieve. Don't oversoak. Skin and put potatoes to boil.

Instead of lamb, use any cooked meats, debone and slice thinly. Slice onion thinly. Pound/crush garlic. Cut baby corn into strips, tomatoes into small wedges. Top and tail mange touts. Slice button mushrooms. When potatoes are ready, cut into bite size chunks. Chop coriander. Prepare spice paste. Break eggs into a bowl, beat well; add 1 tbsp rich soya and coriander. Measure out all other ingredients and take to marshalling area.

Heat 3 tbsp oil in pan/wok. Pour in beaten egg and fry till brown on both sides. Remove from oil and cool. Cut into small strips for garnishing. Pour in remaining oil and saute garlic, onion till brown. Put in spice paste and saute till fragrant. If using uncooked meat, put in at this juncture and saute till cooked. Then put in beansprouts, mange touts, baby corns, mushrooms and tomatoes. Turn heat down. Put in vermicelli, tomato ketchup, soya sauce and salt. Mix thoroughly till vermicelli has taken on the colour of the spice. Put in potatoes. Remove entirely from pan/wok. Just before serving, sprinkle egg strips on top.

SAVOURY POTATO CROQUET
PEGEDIL (Ref: Cs 8)

Crispy potato croquets lovely as a snack
Preparation Time: 15 mins. Cooking Time: 10 mins
(2 persons)

INGREDIENTS
400 gm potato
1 onion
2 cloves garlic
2 eggs
1 dsp gr. coriander
1 dsp gr. cummin
1 tsp gr. black pepper
1 tsp gr. cinnamon
1 dsp cornflour
1 tbsp single cream
2 oz butter
a sprig of coriander
6 tbsp veg oil

MAIN UTENSIL
pan/wok

METHOD
Skin and boil potatoes then mash. Use leftovers if you have. (If your mash contains salt and butter omit the following.) Mash with butter, single cream and salt. Put mash in mixing bowl.

Dice onions. Pound/crush garlic. Chop up fresh coriander finely. Separate the yolks from the whites. Put the onion, garlic, fresh coriander, egg yolks and spices into the mash. Mix well. Take a dessertspoonful of mixture and form into croquets. Makes 12.

Heat oil in pan/wok over medium heat. Just before putting the croquets in the oil, dip in egg white until fully coated. Then gently slip into oil. Approx 2 mins on each side. Make sure that you do not put too many in at one time because the egg white will spread and attach itself to neighbouring croquets. Serve hot or cold, on its own or with other dishes.

Note: If you like, you can also grill rather than fry.

> **VEGETARIAN CONVERSION**
> *Not necessary.*

VERMICELLI IN SAVOURY COCONUT MILK
LAKSA LEMAK (Ref: Cs 9)

Something piquant and tasty for a mouthwatering snack
Preparation Time: 15 mins. Cooking Time: 20 mins
(4 persons)

INGREDIENTS
200 gm vermicelli
200 gm prawns *V
20 quail eggs
1 block tofu
1 onion
3 cloves garlic
1 lemon grass
4 tomatoes

} *Put in blender and add a little water to get a smooth mixture = Mix 'A'*

2 tbsp hot chilli powder
1 dsp gr. cummin
1 tsp coriander

} *Add a few drops of water to make into a paste, = Mix 'B'*

11/2 tbsp roasted groundnuts + 4 toasted almonds
200 gm beansprouts
50 gm sweet/ordinary basil
2 bay leaves
800 ml veg stock
6 tbsp coconut cream
2 tbsp single cream
2 tbsp sesame oil + 2 tbsp veg oil
salt to taste

MAIN UTENSIL
pan, saucepan, 4 individual bowls

METHOD
Put vermicelli in a large bowl and pour hot, boiling water over it to hydrate. Drain. Peel prawns. Boil quail eggs till hard-boiled. Cool, then shell. Slice tofu into 1 x 6 cm strips. Cut tomatoes into wedges. Prepare Mixes 'A' and 'B'. Pound groundnuts and almonds together. Chop up basil.

Put pan over heat with 2 tbsp oil. Fry the sliced tofu on both sides till brown. Remove from oil. Put saucepan with some water, bring to the boil, then blanch beansprouts. Discard water. Divide the vermicelli and beansprouts in equal amounts in the individual bowls.

Put saucepan over heat again and put in Mix 'A', stir till excess liquid dries up. Pour in sesame oil and saute till brown. Put in Mix 'B' and saute till fragrant. Pour in veg stock and put in tomatoes, bay leaves and salt. Bring to the boil, then put in prawns, quail eggs, tofu, nuts, coconut cream and single cream. Turn heat down. When tomatoes have completely disintegrated, remove from heat. To serve, 'soup' must be very hot. Pour equal amounts into the bowls of vermicelli to completely cover it. Sprinkle with chopped basil.

> **VEGETARIAN CONVERSION**
> **V, Put in 5 chunks of Quorn instead of prawns.*

SINGAPOREAN SAVOURY CARROT CAKE
CHYE TOW KWAY (Ref: Cs 10)

Whether steamed or fried, this is a wonderful snack
Preparation Time: 10 mins. Cooking Time: 20 mins
(4 persons)

INGREDIENTS

200 gm mouli
250 gm carrots
} *Or 450 gm carrots, if mouli is unavailable*

200 gm rice flour
1 dsp dried mixed herbs
1 dsp dried veg stock
150 ml water
100 ml veg oil
salt to taste
To Fry:
5 eggs
3 cloves garlic
11/2 tbsp chilli powder (Make into thick paste)
50 gm fresh coriander
2 tbsp light soya sauce
5 tbsp sesame oil

MAIN UTENSIL
Flan dish 3 cm x 22 cm, saucepan, steamer, large pan/wok

VEGETARIAN CONVERSION
Not necessary.

METHOD
Put steamer to boil over heat. Grease flan dish.

Grate mouli/carrot in small strips. Sieve flour and salt into a mixing bowl. Pour water in and mix until there are no lumps. Put in oil, veg stock and dried herbs. Stir well.

Put saucepan on another hob and put in grated mouli/carrot with just a little water to wet them. Stir evenly, then pour in batter. Keep on stirring until batter thickens and changes colour. Remove from heat and scoop into flan dish. Level off nicely and put in steamer and steam for 15 mins. (When cooked, cut into squares, remove and serve on plates with chilli sauce.)

To Fry: Prepare other ingredients while cake is in the steamer. Pound/crush garlic. Prepare chilli paste. Chop up fresh coriander. Break eggs into a bowl and beat well; add chopped coriander, 1 tbsp light soya sauce.

When carrot cake is ready, cut into approx 6cm squares.

Heat sesame oil in pan/wok. When fragrant, put in garlic and chilli paste. saute till slightly brown. Put in carrot cake squares and turn each square to coat well with the chilli. Pour in egg mixture, (if necessary, add a little more oil.) Allow underside to brown before turning over. Break cake/omelette into smaller pieces so that they can be browned and made crispier. Sprinkle the rest of the light soya sauce over the cake. Mix well, then remove from oil and serve hot.

Note: If preferred, add 250 gm boiled prawns for added flavour.

FRIED BEANCURD IN PEANUT SOYA
TAUHU GORENG (Ref No: Cs 11)

Bean Curd in a sweet/salty sauce
Preparation Time: 10 mins. Cooking Time: 5 mins
(2 persons)

INGREDIENTS
1 block extra firm beancurd
1/2 onion
3 cloves garlic
1 tbsp chilli powder
100 gm beansprouts
1/2 cucumber approx 12 cm
10 tbsp roasted peanuts
3 tbsp rich soya sauce
1 dsp honey
1 dsp malt vinegar
100 ml veg stock
6 tbsp veg oil

MAIN UTENSIL
pan/wok, saucepan

VEGETARIAN CONVERSION
Not necessary.

METHOD
Slice into the thickness of beancurd to get two large slices. Dice onion. Pound/crush garlic. Add a few drops of water to chilli to make a thick paste. Pound peanuts roughly. Cut across cucumber to get small wedges. Measure out the other ingredients and take to marshalling area.

Heat oil in pan and fry the two pieces of beancurd till brown on both sides. Slice each beancurd into two large strips, then cut across to get small squares. Put each set in two separate serving dishes. Take pan off heat, put saucepan with some water, bring to the boil and blanch beansprouts. Divide the beansprouts equally over the beancurds. Do the same with the cucumber.

Scoop out most of the oil in the pan to leave about 2 tbsp Put over heat. Put in onion and garlic and saute till onion is soft. Add chilli paste and saute till fragrant. Pour in stock, bring to the boil. Then put in peanuts, soya sauce, honey and vinegar. Stir continuously till sauce thickens completely. Pour over beancurd pieces. Serve hot or cold.

GLOSSARY OF RECIPE NAMES

Page:	Ref. No:	Name	Language	Meaning
14	Mb 1	Keema	*Malay*	Just a name
14	Mb 2	Rendang	*Malay*	Just a name
15	Mb 3	Timpra Lembu	*Malay*	Timpra = soya sauce with lemon, Lembu = beef
15	Mb 4	Kofta	*Indian*	mixed minced
16	Mb 5	–	–	–
16	Mb 6	Gu Bak Char	*Teochew*	Gu Bak = beef, Char = fried
17	Mb 7	Kari Lembu	*Malay*	Kari = curry
17	Mb 8	Gu Bak Char Chye	*Teochew*	Chye = vegetable
18	Mc 1	Ayam Lemak Pekat	*Malay*	Ayam = chicken, Lemak = rich/coconut Pekat = thick sauce
18	Mc 2	Ayam Goreng	*Malay*	Goreng = fried
19	Mc 3	Sayap Bakar	*Malay*	Sayap = wings, Bakar = barbecue
19	Mc 4	Sambal Ayam	*Malay*	Sambal = chilli sauce
20	Mc 5	Ayam Bakar Dalam		Dalam = In, Asam = tamarind
20	Mc 6	–	–	–
21	Ml 1	Kwa Char	*Teochew*	Kwa = liver
21	Ml 2	Kambing Masak	*Malay*	Kambing =lamb, Masak = cook, Merah = red
22	Ml 3	Kerumak Kambing	*Malay*	Kerumak = mild sauce
22	Ml 4	Kambing Bakar	*Malay*	Bakar = barbecue
23	Ml 5	Kambing Dalam Bawang Puteh	*Malay*	Bawang Puteh = garlic
23	Mp 1	Babi Pongteh	*Straits Chinese*	Babi = pork, Pongteh = just a name
24	Mp 2	Kari serani	*Malay*	Serani = Eurasian
24	Mp 3	Bak Ee Chwere	*Teochew*	Bak Ee = meat balls, Chwere = steamed
25	Mp 4	Rempah Babi	*Straits Chinese*	Rempah = dry spices, Babi = pork
25	Mp 5	Sambal Babi	*Straits Chinese*	(same as malay)
26	Sf 1	Chwere Her	*Teochew*	Her = fish
26	Sf 2	Ikan Pari Bakar	*Malay*	Ikan Pari = skate
27	Sf 3	Ikan Tomato	*Malay*	Ikan = fish
27	Sf 4	Otak-Otak	*Malay*	Otak = brains (original ingredients)
28	Sf 5	Sambal Ikan	*Malay*	Fish in chilli
28	Sf 6	Chilli Udang	*Malay*	Udang = prawns
29	Sf 7	Kari Ikan	*Malay*	Fish curry
29	Sf 8	Ikan Pari Masak Asam Pedas	*Malay*	Pedas = hot
30	Sf 9	Sambal Sardine	*Malay*	Sardine in chilli

Page:	Ref. No:	Name	Language	Meaning
30	Sf 10	Sardine Goreng	*Malay*	Fried sardine
31	Sf 11	Ikan Pari Panggang	*Malay*	Pangang = baked
31	Sf 12	–	–	–
32	E 1	Kari Telor	*Malay*	Telor = egg
32	E 2	Telor Goreng	*Malay*	Telor Goreng Dengan Daging = omelette, Dengan= with
33	E 3	Telor Goreng Dengan Chilli	*Malay*	Omelette with chilli
33	E 4	Telor Dalam Kuah Satay	*Malay*	Kuah Satay = satay sauce
34	E 5	Telor Goreng Dengan Udang kechil	*Malay*	Udang Kechil = small prawns
34	E 6	Sambal Telor	*Malay*	Eggs in chilli sauce
35	V 1	Taugeh Goreng	*Malay*	Taugeh = beansprouts (also in chinese)
35	V 2	Sayur Champur	*Malay*	Sayur = vegetables Champur = mixed
36	V 3	Gado-Gado	*Malay*	Gado = fight, now just a name
36	V 4	Ubi Goreng	*Malay*	Ubi = potato
37	V 5	Kobis Goreng	*Malay*	Kobis = cabbage
37	V 6	Achar	*Indian*	Achar = pickle
38	V 7	Sayur Dal	*Indian*	Dal = lentils
38	V 8	–	–	–
39	V 9	–	–	–
39	V 10	–	–	–
40	V 11	Bindi Dalam Kunyik	*Malay*	Bindi = okra, Kunyik = turmeric
40	V 12	–	–	–
41	Sp 1	Sup Kambing	*Malay*	Lamb soup
41	Sp 2	Bak Tng	*Teochew*	Bak = pork, Tng = clear soup
42	Sp 3	Sup Ayam	*Malay*	Chicken soup
42	Sp 4	Sup Ikan	*Malay*	Fish soup
43	Sp 5	Hoy/Bak Tng	*Teochew*	Hoy = crab
44	Cs 1	Satay Babi	*Straits Chinese*	Pork satay
45	Cs 2	Roti Jala	*Malay*	Roti = bread, Jala = net
45	Cs 3	Pai Kwat	*Cantonese*	Ribs
46	Cs 4	Popia Goreng	*Straits Chinese*	Popia = spring rolls
46	Cs 5	Her Moey	*Teochew*	Moey = porridge
47	Cs 6	Nasi Goreng	*Malay*	Nasi = rice
47	Cs 7	Bee Hoon Goreng	*Malay*	Bee Hoon = vermicelli
48	Cs 8	Pegedil	*Malay*	Just a name
48	Cs 9	Laksa Lemak	*Straits Chinese*	Laksa = thick, rice noodles
49	Cs 10	Chye Tow Kway	*Teochew*	Chye Tow = carrot, Kway = cake
49	Cs 11	Tauhu Goreng	*Malay*	Tauhu = beancurd